# FLYING BOATS

## AIR TRAVEL IN THE GOLDEN AGE

# CHARLES WOODLEY

# FLYING BOATS

## AIR TRAVEL IN THE GOLDEN AGE

The History Press

First published 2018

The History Press
The Mill, Brimscombe Port
Stroud, Gloucestershire, GL5 2QG
www.thehistorypress.co.uk

British Library Cataloguing in Publication Data.
A catalogue record for this book is available from the British Library.

ISBN 978 0 7509 7014 3

Typesetting and origination by The History Press
Printed and bound in Great Britain by TJ International Ltd

# CONTENTS

# AUTHOR'S NOTE

Throughout this book I have used the place names in use during the period covered. Many of them have changed in the intervening years and their modern-day versions are as follows:

| | |
|---|---|
| Belgian Congo | now Democratic Republic of Congo |
| Calcutta | now Kolkata |
| Canton Island | now Kanton, part of Kiribati |
| French Equatorial Africa | now several independent countries under the name of Union of Central African Republics |
| Jiwani | was in India, now in Pakistan |
| Karachi | was in India, now in Pakistan |
| Malakal | was in Sudan, now in South Sudan |
| Malaya | now Malaysia |
| Northern Rhodesia | now Zambia |
| Nyasaland | now Malawi |
| Rangoon | now Yangon, in Burma/Myanmar |
| Salisbury | was in Rhodesia, now Harare in Zimbabwe |
| Sumatra | was in Dutch East Indies, now in East Java province of Indonesia |
| Surabaya | was in Dutch East Indies, now in East Java province of Indonesia |
| Tanganyika | now Tanzania |
| Trucial Oman | was part of the British Empire, now part of the United Arab Emirates |
| Wadi Halfa | was in Sudan, now in South Sudan |

# ACKNOWLEDGEMENTS

Many people and organisations have kindly assisted me in the preparation of this book by sending me images, memories, information and good wishes for its success. They are listed below with my thanks, but if I have inadvertently omitted anyone I apologise and thank them once again.

Chris Smith at the Solent Sky Museum
Ron Cuskelly at the Queensland Air Museum
David Cheek at GKN Aerospace
Aimee Alexander at the Poole Flying Boat Celebration
Barry O'Neill at the Foynes Flying Boat and Maritime Museum
Dave Thaxter at the British Caledonian website
Judy Noller at Ansett Public Relations
David Crotty, Curator, Qantas Heritage Collection
Doug Miller, webmaster at the Pan Am Historical Foundation
Kim Baker
Peter Maxfield
Felicity Laws
Elizabeth Malson
Beryl Cawood
Hilary Adams
Jeremy Cutler
Les Ellyatt
Peter Savage
Janet Beazley
Chris Mooney
Sue Marks

Paul Sheehan

Anthony Leyfeldt

Frank Stamford for his Lord Howe Island flying boats images

Jenny Scott at the State Library of South Australia

My friend Raul in Buenos Aires for finding me rare South American flying boat images

Amy Rigg at The History Press for her continuing faith in my abilities and her encouragement

And, of course, my wife Hazel.

# INTRODUCTION

At the beginning of the 1930s Britain ruled over an empire that spanned the globe, but travel between the mother country and its far-flung overseas possessions was a laborious and time-consuming process. The journey to Karachi (then in India) took some seven days and involved transfers between trains, ships and aircraft along the way. The need for speedier transportation of the all-important mail and the few passengers that accompanied it led to the setting up of the Empire Air Mail Scheme, whereby all mail to and from the Empire would be transported by air throughout at a government-subsidised standard rate. In order to accommodate the anticipated volume, larger and more modern airliners would be needed, and in response to a request for proposals the Empire-class flying boat designs emerged. Built by established flying boat manufacturer Short Bros, these would be capable of carrying the mail as well as a small number of cosseted passengers all the way to Africa, the Middle East and India in new standards of comfort. The lack of land airports and night-flying facilities along the routes would be bypassed by using marine facilities with long water take-off areas, and all flying would take place during the daylight hours, with the passengers spending the nights in luxury hotels or company-owned houseboats, all included in the fare. The introduction of the Empire-class flying boats by Britain's state airline Imperial Airways certainly ushered in new standards of passenger comfort and attentive service, but the aircraft were still far from fast, the journey could be uncomfortably bumpy at times, and the fares were beyond the reach of the average working man.

In the meantime, on the other side of the Atlantic, the USA's overseas 'flag carrier' airline Pan American Airways was operating smaller Sikorsky flying boats to the Caribbean islands, the West Indies, and down the coastline of South America. The airline's founder, Juan Trippe, had more ambitious plans though, for flying boat services across the Pacific to the Far East via Hawaii. Before such plans could become a reality, however, staging posts would have to be constructed on a string of small islands such as Wake and Midway along the route. The airline set to and installed refuelling facilities for its aircraft and luxury hotel accommodation for its passengers at these stopover points, and in due course the services were inaugurated, using a new generation of giant Martin and Boeing Clipper flying boats.

Both Imperial Airways and Pan American then turned their attention to the much trickier proposition of North Atlantic operations between Europe and the USA. The route involved battling against inclement weather conditions for much of the journey, and experiments were carried out to determine the practicality of in-flight refuelling to give the necessary range. Some experimental services were operated by both carriers in 1940, but further progress with operations across the Atlantic and the Pacific were then disrupted by the Second World War, which saw the airlines operating according to wartime priorities on behalf of their governments.

When commercial airline services resumed after the war, much had changed. During the hostilities new land airfields with long concrete runways had been constructed for use by large four-engined bombers. Both the airfields and the aircraft could be adapted to fulfil short-term airline needs, and the commercial flying boats soon became redundant. Britain's new national airline, BOAC (which had replaced Imperial Airways in 1940), kept faith with its flying boats for a few more years, operating them on popular and well-patronised services from Southampton to South Africa until late-1950, when they were replaced by landplanes. Many of the retired BOAC flying boats then found a new home with Aquila Airways, flying holiday services to the island of Madeira, which at that time had no land airport. They were to serve this route, and others to Las Palmas and the Isle of Capri, well for several years. Other flying boats were operated in the South Pacific area, carrying passengers to romantic destinations such as Tahiti and Lord Howe Island, and they also gave useful service in South America and along Norway's northern coastline, but they eventually reached the end of their operating lives. No replacements were built, and the era of the passenger flying boat passed into history. This book sets out to do justice to an age of glamorous, unhurried air travel, unrecognisable to most of today's air travellers, but sorely missed by some.

# 1

# IMPERIAL AIRWAYS AND THE EMPIRE AIR MAIL SCHEME

On 1 April 1924 the British airline Imperial Airways came into being as the product of the merger of Handley Page Air Transport, The Instone Airline, Daimler Airways, and British Marine Air Navigation. These independent airlines had been unable to compete effectively against the state-backed carriers of countries such as Germany and the Netherlands, and their incorporation into a British government-subsidised 'flag carrier' was seen as the key to operating efficiencies and future expansion to serve the global outposts of the British Empire. In the late 1920s the fastest journey to Karachi (then in British India) took seven days and entailed a landplane flight from Croydon airport to Basle followed by rail travel to Genoa, where a flying boat was boarded for the air journey to Alexandria in Egypt. From there another train conveyed passengers to Cairo, where they embarked on a DH.66 landplane for the final leg to Karachi. Even in 1934 passengers wishing to travel speedily between London and Athens had to first fly from Croydon to Paris by landplane before boarding a train for the 950-mile leg to Brindisi and then switching to a Short S.17 Kent flying boat to get to Athens. Part of the reason for these convoluted itineraries was Italy's reluctance to grant overflying rights to Imperial Airways, and it took until 1936 for these to be negotiated. The way was then clear to make plans for travel entirely by air to all parts of the Empire. A major boost to these ambitions came with the government announcement in December 1934 of the Empire Air Mail Scheme (later renamed the Empire Air Mail Programme), intended to speed up communications between the territories of the Empire and the mother country. From 1937 Imperial Airways would receive a subsidy to carry nearly all of the mail to South Africa, India, Australia and New Zealand and other

Imperial Airways Short S.23 G-ADUZ *Cygnus* unloading at her moorings. (via author)

Empire territories at the same rates as surface post. It was calculated that in order to carry the anticipated quantities of mail as well as some passengers the Imperial fleet would need to be expanded to be capable of operating four or five flights each week to India, three per week to Singapore and East Africa, and two each week to South Africa and Australia. New and larger aircraft would need to be designed, and the Air Ministry expressed its insistence on these being flying boats, giving as its reasons:

> That neither the government nor Imperial Airways could afford the investment needed to enlarge existing land aerodromes, many of which became unusable during the monsoon season in certain countries.

That flying-boats provided a greater sense of security during flights over long stretches of water and would also be able to circumvent problems over the granting of landing rights in certain countries by flying more direct routeings, also reducing fuel costs.

That flying-boats would be able to provide greater comfort for passengers, even though the mail would always be given priority for space.

Thus, despite certain economic penalties they would incur, the flying boat was seen as the best option for the new services. It was agreed that the government would provide an annual subsidy of £750,000, and the Post Office an additional £900,000, for the carriage of the mail, plus an extra £75,000 to cover the cost of extra flights over the Christmas period. Imperial Airways also managed to persuade the Admiralty to provide all the launches, refuelling tenders, and mooring facilities along the routes free of charge.

In order to compete with the speedy landplanes of its competitors, such as the Douglas DC-2s of the Dutch airline KLM, Imperial needed spacious

Mailbags being unloaded from Imperial Airways Short S.23 G-ADHM *Caledonia* into a launch. (via author)

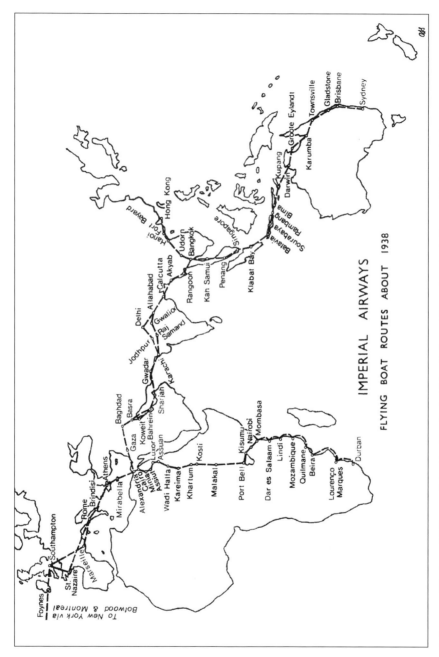

IMPERIAL AIRWAYS

FLYING BOAT ROUTES ABOUT 1938

A diagram of the Imperial Airways flying-boat routes to Africa, India and through to Australia c. 1938. (via author)

flying boats that could offer its passengers unrivalled comfort and facilities on a par with the ocean liners of the day. In order to get such aircraft into service with the minimum of delay, Imperial Airways invited Short Bros of Rochester in Kent to submit a design for an improved version of its existing Kent flying boat, which could also meet an RAF requirement for a long-range maritime patrol aircraft. The result was the Short S.23, an all-metal high-wing monoplane of clean lines with a deep hull, single tailfin and rudder, and fixed wing-tip floats. The aircraft's interior was divided into two decks, and power was to be provided by four 740bhp Bristol Pegasus Xc piston engines. Imperial was sufficiently impressed by the design to order twenty-eight examples at a cost of around £45,000 each before a prototype had even flown. The Air Ministry also ordered a prototype of the

A 1939 Imperial Airways advertisement showing its Empire flying-boat service frequencies before the Second World War intervened.
(via author)

### 40 winks at 180 miles per hour

### ALL THE WAY
### to INDIA by
### EMPIRE FLYING-BOAT

Already one service a week, and soon all services will be by the famous *Empire* flying-boats all the way, giving pullman comfort in the air — promenade — smoker — the world's most comfortable armchairs. The fare includes tips and everything, except drinks

# IMPERIAL AIRWAYS

Imperial Airways Ltd., Airway Terminus, S.W.1; Airways House, Charles Street, S.W.1; VICtoria 2211 (Day & Night), or travel agents.
Imperial Airways is agent in Great Britain for Belgian Air Lines, German Airways, Swissair and Railway Air Services.

*Kindly mention " Flight " when corresponding with advertisers.*

An Imperial Airways magazine advertisement for their newly introduced Empire flying-boats on the route to India. (via author)

military S.25 version (later to become famous in RAF service as the Short Sunderland). Imperial had originally wanted to give its machines the class name the Imperial Flying boat, but soon changed this to the Empire Flying boat. Construction of the order commenced at Rochester in 1935, and the first example, registered as G-ADHL and carrying the name *Canopus* (all of the Imperial fleet were to be allocated names beginning with C and to become known as the C Class), first flew from the River Medway on

3 July 1936. On the following day an official 'maiden flight' was staged in front of the entire workforce. No aircraft of such size and complexity had been built before by Britain, and the press were allowed to inspect the almost fully fitted-out *Canopus* shortly afterwards. One reporter described the aircraft in rather Jules Verne or H.G. Wells prose as follows:

> No aeroplane yet built has given that same sense of freedom to move and breathe. Every saloon has a breadth and height in excess of the best that rail or road transport can offer ... The forward part of the deck is fully occupied with the gear of control navigation and communication. The instruments and

The promenade deck cabin on an Imperial Airways Empire flying-boat. (via author)

Forward saloon of an Empire flying-boat. (via author)

A cutaway view of the new Empire flying-boats used on the Imperial Airways and Qantas services to Australia. (Qantas Heritage Collection)

the apparatus, from the loop aerial of the directional wireless to the artificial horizon and the switch for the landing lights, the levers, dials and levels, makes the pilots' compartment a mass of complications, and foreshadows the day when the big aeroplanes, such as certainly will be built for ocean crossings, will need an engine room separate from the bridge.

The Imperial Airways order was later increased to thirty-two examples, plus six more to be delivered to Australia for use by Qantas Empire Airways on services between Singapore and Australia, and two more for completion to long-range S.30 specification for use on trials for possible transatlantic services. After crew training and acceptance trials had been completed, *Canopus* was handed over to Imperial Airways on 20 October 1936. The rest of the fleet followed at intervals of one or two per month. On 22 October *Canopus* set off for Genoa for service on trans-Mediterranean routes. The first scheduled service to be operated by an Empire flying-boat left Alexandria for Brindisi via Mirabella and Athens on 30 October, and on 4 January 1937 the route was extended onwards from Brindisi to Marseilles.

The flying boats were more than just aircraft that could land on water, they were boats that flew, and many nautical terms were used to describe their structure and operation. Passengers boarded via a forward door on the port side of the lower deck and entered the lobby area, which was curtained off from the passenger cabins. Forward of this was a compartment containing seven seats and lightweight stowable meal tables. This cabin featured a large rectangular window and was at first used as a smoking cabin. The décor consisted of bottle-green walls and white ceilings, and the seats were upholstered in dark green leather. Aft of the entrance door was a central corridor offset slightly to port, with the galley and stewards' pantry to one side and two toilets on the other. Continuing aft, the corridor led to the midships, or 'spar' cabin, which seated three passengers in the daytime and could be converted to bunk accommodation for overnight flights. Further aft along the corridor small steps led into the promenade cabin, which was fitted with seats for eight passengers on the starboard side. On the opposite

The Imperial Airways Short S.23 flying-boat G-ADHM *Caledonia* at her moorings with a launch alongside the forward door. (via author)

side there was ample space for passengers to stand and lean on an elbow rail whilst observing the scenery and wildlife passing below through the large window area. Once again, if night flying proved necessary, the seats in this area could be converted into four bunks. Moving rearward again, a small step upwards brought one to the rear door on the port side, and up another step was the rear cabin with accommodation for six seated passengers or four in bunks. In practice, the sleeping berths were almost never used on scheduled services as full night-flying facilities were not to be installed along the routes for some years to come. The rear cabins were furnished with grey carpeting and dove-grey ceilings, with the walls and seat coverings in bottle green. Also on the lower deck were compartments for luggage and freight, and in the nose of the aircraft was a mooring compartment with such nautical accoutrements as an anchor, boat hooks and a retractable mooring bollard.

Imperial Airways Empire flying-boat G-AETX *Ceres* on the water near Mombasa. (via author)

Underneath the decking were bilge pumps for disposing of any water that seeped into the hull. The upper deck was accessed by a ladder from the stewards' pantry, and was normally out of bounds to passengers. On the flight deck, or 'bridge', sat the captain and first officer. Behind them, and facing aft, was the wireless operator. He was also responsible for mooring the aircraft. To perform this task he had to descend to the mooring compartment via a small hatch in the floor between the pilots' seats. Aft of the wireless operator's station was the mail storage area. Towards the rear of the upper deck was the desk of the flight clerk, whose many duties included the preparation of the aircraft's load sheets and trim sheets, the compilation of passenger lists, the handling of freight consignments, the customs and immigration procedures, and the safekeeping of the inoculation certificates of the passengers and crew. In the event of overnight flights he was also expected to descend to the lower deck and help the stewards to make up the bunks using bedding stored in the aft portion of the wing box, above the promenade cabin. From mid 1937 his rather inconveniently sited workstation was relocated downstairs into what had previously been the forward smoking compartment. He was also given the grander job title of purser. The Empire flying boats did not carry an engineering officer or navigating officer, their duties being carried out by the first officer. On top of the flight deck was a mast from which the appropriate ensign could be flown during stopovers. The pilots had to put up with some discomfort on these aircraft. The controls for the Sperry autopilot were located on the captain's side and tended to leak oil onto his left trouser leg, and when it rained the leaky flight deck roof dripped water onto both pilots. The passengers were always looked after by male stewards, mostly recruited from the ocean liners of the Cunard steamship company. Imperial Airways was against the employment of stewardesses on any of its aircraft. As the company put it:

> This curious hybrid nursemaid-cum-waitress was not the best way of putting the passengers at their ease … Our aerial stewards are men of a new calling. They have to be, since much is expected of them. In less than an hour a couple of flying stewards can serve six courses, with wines, to between thirty and forty people.

The first C-class scheduled service was operated from Alexandria to Brindisi by *Canopus* on 30 October 1936, fewer than sixteen weeks after she had been launched. In December of that year sister ship *Caledonia* was

The Imperial Airways Short S.23 G-ADUW *Castor* at Gladstone, Australia. (via author)

flown out to Alexandria with 5 tons of the Christmas mail on board. She continued onwards to India on route-proving duties. On her way back to Britain she covered the leg from Alexandria to Marseilles in just over eleven hours, and flew onwards to Hythe, near Southampton, in four hours. In January 1937 *Castor* and *Centaurus* commenced a regular series of flights from Hythe to Marseilles and Alexandria via Lake Bracciano (for Rome), Brindisi and Athens.

Hythe had been selected by Imperial Airways for use as a temporary UK flying boat terminal in 1934, after serious consideration had also been given to the use of Langstone Harbour at Portsmouth, while the site for a permanent base was still to be decided. A maintenance base was also set up at Hythe, in sheds rented from Vickers Supermarine Aviation. To get to the terminal from London, passengers travelled on the 0830hrs train from Waterloo Station to Southampton in a dedicated Pullman railway carriage proudly bearing the title 'Imperial Airways Empire Service'. Also attached to the train was a special guard's van in which the aircraft's flight clerk processed the luggage details and compiled the load sheet en route to Southampton. Imperial was to experience difficulties in getting the passengers there in time for the mid-morning flight using this train, and the decision was taken

An Imperial Airways magazine advertisement for their new Empire-class flying-boats, featuring the promenade deck cabin. (via author)

to transport them down the previous evening and put them up in a hotel overnight. In the morning the passengers would clear customs at Berth 50 at Southampton and be transferred to the aircraft moored off Hythe in one of the many launches that had been built for Imperial by the British Power Boat Company. Boarding the launch and then transferring to the flying boat was a tricky procedure in any kind of rough weather, particularly for the less agile passengers, and operations were later to be moved to the more sheltered No. 9 Berth while pontoons were constructed at 101 Berth. Once this work was done the flying boats could be winched tail-first into moorings at the quayside, eliminating the need for the launch transfer. In late 1938 the pontoons were to be moved to Berth 108, where a two-storey wooden terminal building named 'Imperial House' was erected. Things did not always run smoothly on these services. On 6 February 1937 Captain H.W.C. 'Jimmy' Algar was in command of *Castor* for a service from Hythe to Alexandria. On board were eight passengers, a ton of mail and five large cases containing bullion. One more passenger was booked to join the flight at Marseilles, and another at Brindisi. The take-off from Hythe was uneventful, but ten minutes later the aircraft returned, suffering from oiled up spark plugs. The plug change took longer than expected, and by the time the aircraft was serviceable again it had become apparent that Brindisi could not be reached that night. The passengers were taken off to spend the night at the Lawn Hotel in Hythe and police were called in to guard the bullion. Rough weather made operations impossible the next day, and so it was not until 0720hrs on 8 February that the flight eventually departed. On 24 March Imperial Airways lost C-class flying boat *Capricornus* in a fatal accident. The aircraft was en route from Hythe to Marseilles when it struck a hillside 12 miles south-west of Macon in France. It was carrying just a single passenger, plus a consignment of bullion and the first mail scheduled to be transported all the way to Australia by air. The first officer was thrown out of the aircraft on impact and was the only survivor.

From 15 May 1937 the C-class flying boats operated through to Africa, although at first only as far as Kisumu, a freshwater port on Lake Victoria and Kenya's third-largest city. About fifteen minutes before arriving there the aircraft crossed the equator, and to mark the crossing of this invisible feature the Imperial pilots used to waggle the wings or dip the aircraft's nose, and it was customary for each passenger to be presented with a certificate signed by the captain. As the flying boat fleet was expanded, the route was extended through to Durban, with *Centurion* departing Hythe on 29 June 1937 for

The Imperial Airways Short S.23 G-AETX being worked on outdoors at Rose Bay, Sydney, while the new hangar takes shape in the background. (Qantas Heritage Collection)

the Sudan, Northern Rhodesia, Nyasaland and South Africa with 3,500lb of unsurcharged mail at the surface post rate of 1½d for a half-ounce letter and 1d for a postcard. Imperial was not allowed to operate all the way through to the Cape as the South African authorities had specified that only South African Airways could fly into Cape Town. Until 1937 the usual mode of travel to South Africa had been aboard the Union Castle Line's weekly mail steamer from Southampton, which took two weeks to reach the Cape. By September of that year Imperial Airways was flying twice-weekly to South Africa, and produced a thirty-page booklet for passengers titled 'Through Africa by the Empire Flying boat'. This traced the entire route from Hythe and described the many points of interest along the way. Over Africa the pilots often descended to low altitudes to offer passengers excellent views of herds of elephants, plus rhinos and giraffes on the plains below. A favourite spot for viewing hippos was just below Murchison Falls at the northern end of Lake Albert in Uganda. The one-way fare to South Africa in 1937 was £125, which included all meals, overnight accommodation and tips, and was based on the criteria that the total weight of each passenger and luggage would not exceed 221lb. For this price the flying boat passengers enjoyed far more space and more attentive cabin service than today's economy-class passengers are accustomed to, although the low cruising altitude of the unpressurised aircraft did mean that turbulence was quite often encountered. To cope with the extreme temperatures at stopover points in Africa, Imperial Airways advised its passengers to take the opportunity to purchase topees, or sun helmets, from the local traders. A lady passenger travelling to Durban aboard *Castor* in 1937 kept a journal of her experiences, including the overnight stops and the very early departures from them:

A Qantas promotional photo of the interior of the passenger compartments of the Short S.23 Empire-class flying-boat. (Qantas Heritage Collection)

**20th August 1937.** Departed Waterloo for Southampton at 1930hrs in Imperial Airways Pullman carriage. Stayed overnight in the South Western Hotel.

**21st August 1937.** Roused at 0645hrs and taken to docks by hotel bus. Took off for Marseilles at 0830hrs. Coffee or Bovril served at 1030hrs. Arrived at Marseilles at 1230hrs and departed again at 1400hrs bound for Rome. Luncheon served on board. Arrived 1630hrs at Lake Bracciano. One-hour drive by Imperial Airways bus to Grande Hotel de Russie in Rome for tea, dinner, and overnight accommodation.

**22nd August 1937.** Roused at 0345hrs and left hotel at 0445hrs. Took off at 0600hrs for Brindisi, where arrived at 0900hrs. After departure from there at 0945hrs, morning tea was served at 1000hrs. Next stop Athens. After 30 minute halt there, lunch was served on board at 1430hrs. Arrived Alexandria at 1730hrs. Disembarked for tea in customs houses, and dinner and overnight stay at Hotel Cecil. Time for stroll with fellow passengers after dinner.

**23rd August 1937.** Early departure for Cairo, arriving there at 0745hrs. Breakfast on the deck of an Imperial Airways houseboat before departure for Luxor. After arrival there at 1115hrs, taken for trip on the Nile by motor launch, with iced coffee being served. Then flight onwards to Wadi Halfa and Khartoum. Long drive there to Grand Hotel for overnight stay.

**24th August 1937.** 0600hrs departure for Malakal, arriving at 0845hrs. Ashore for breakfast at the Imperial Airways accommodation, a very nice house on the river bank. Then onwards to Port Bell and a drive to Kampala for overnight stay.

**25th August 1937.** Back to Port Bell for 0600hrs take-off for Kisumu. Ashore for breakfast at the Kisumu Hotel and a walk around the town before onward flight to Mombasa, arriving there at 1315hrs. Ashore again for lunch at the Manor Hotel. Flight onwards to Dar-es-Salaam for overnight stop.

**26th August 1937.** Flight from Dar-es-Salaam to Lindi, Tanganyika, and on to Beira, Mozambique, arriving at 1645hrs. Overnight accommodation at Savoy Hotel. Not impressed. No private bathroom.

**27th August 1937.** Final day's travel, from Beira to Lourenco Marques and on to Durban, arriving at 1330hrs.

Imperial Airways encouraged its captains to leave the flight deck to converse with their passengers at suitable times. During the Coronation of King George VI on 12 May 1937 Captain Powell joined his passengers on the promenade deck of *Courtier* to propose the Loyal Toast. Then, along with other passengers in flight aboard *Castor* and *Cassiopeia*, they listened to the Coronation service from London on their aircraft's wireless sets. In its publicity material Imperial Airways described its C-class flying boats as providing 'the most effortless and luxurious travel the world has ever seen'. The airline was particularly proud of its patented 'Imperial Airways Adjustable Chair', describing it as 'by far the most comfortable chair in the world, an exclusive to Imperial Airways' and declaring that 'at the touch of a power-operated lever, without leaving your seat you can adjust these wonderful chairs from a 'sit-up lunch table' position to a reclining afternoon-nap position'. Another feature of the chair was its ability to double up as a life-preserver if the worst happened. Much was made of the flying boat's advertised cruising speed of 200mph, although in service this proved to be nearer 145mph. The heating system was not particularly efficient, and few crews could master the art of getting it to perform properly. Passengers complaining of the cold at cruising altitude were issued with blankets and foot muffs. The Empire flying boats were prone to taking on water, and before each flight an engineer would go around each rivet line, tightening up where necessary and coating it with beeswax to make it more watertight.

During 1937 a survey flight to Singapore was made in preparation for the extension of the route network through to the Far East. On a more sombre note, the year was also marked by the loss of three flying boats in accidents. In addition to the previously mentioned loss of *Capricornus*, *Courtier* was destroyed when a newly promoted captain misjudged his height on approach for landing and crashed into Phaleron Bay near Athens. After this accident, in which three passengers were drowned, the Air Ministry made the provision of lap straps in passenger-carrying aircraft compulsory. In December 1937 *Cygnus* stalled on take-off from Brindisi and nosed into the sea, with two passengers drowned. As a result the small roof hatches on the flying boats were replaced by larger escape hatches and push-out windows. The eastbound route network was meanwhile steadily expanding, and by October 1937 it had reached as far as Karachi. The services bound for Karachi usually routed via Kuwait and Dubai, where Imperial had negotiated an arrangement for the rental of a base at Dubai Creek at the rate of over 400 rupees each month. Over the Persian Gulf the air was usually hot and bumpy. After Dubai the route went eastward over the desert, with the aircraft climbing to 8,000ft to clear the mountain ranges. Then it was over the Gulf of Oman to Karachi. This section of the route was subject to monsoons during July and August, with upward convection air currents and much turbulence. Also, tropical storms were frequently encountered during the periods May–June and October–November.

By the end of 1937 Imperial had taken delivery of twenty-two C-class flying boats, and more captains were needed for the fleet. These were recruited from the airline's four existing operations divisions and posted to the newly formed No. 5 Operating Division. Conversion training for Imperial's former landplane crews as well as for new recruits was carried out at Hamble on Southampton Water and also at Richards Bay in South Africa. During a three-month course the trainees had to attend seventeen lectures on such subjects as marine law and the meaning of the various lights and signals displayed by marine craft by day and night. All pilots had already been required to learn Morse code, but now they had to master semaphore as well. Other lectures covered knot tying, the use of Admiralty charts, and the regulations pertaining to towage and salvage. The significance of these particular rules was later to be brought home to one captain who encountered fog and was obliged to alight on the water some distance short of his destination. He accepted the offer of a tow from the skipper of a tug boat, who later sent Imperial Airways a claim for salvage. Practical seamanship training began with batches of three or four trainees learning to handle a 10-ton ketch and motor launches before moving on to Cutty Sark amphibious aircraft and elderly Rangoon or Calcutta flying boats. On these aircraft they learnt the techniques for approaching mooring buoys when the wind was pushing the aircraft in one direction and the tide in another, the deployment of drogues (canvas-covered conical frames used to steady the aircraft while manoeuvring on the water), and the technique of taxiing around in circles while the engines were being warmed up, as the aircraft had no brakes. The differences between landplane and flying boat handling were summed up as:

> Landplane pilots, who had never had to park their aeroplane amongst cars, coaches and lorries, were being trained to handle a flying-boat in the presence of native canoes, Arab dhows and ocean liners. Pilots learnt the vagaries of water landings and how the many variables encountered, wind, currents, swell and tides, could affect their landings.

International regulations decreed that any aircraft proceeding more than 600 miles offshore must carry a licensed first-class navigator, so the possession of this qualification became a prerequisite for promotion to captain. As soon as a flying boat alighted on the water it became by maritime law a boat, and was required to display the flag of its country of origin and another bearing the emblem of its operator.

The passengers on Imperial Airways flying boats were treated to the very best of in-flight catering. Along the route to India they could choose from a breakfast menu offering grapefruit or fruit juices, cereals, omelettes, bacon, bread rolls, marmalade and honey. Later, they were offered midday refreshments, a five-course luncheon (the term 'lunch' was never used on Imperial Airways), and afternoon tea with cakes and sandwiches. A typical luncheon, as served on *Centurion* en route from Lake Naivasha to Durban on 3 February 1938, consisted of potage Jackson, iced asparagus, fricassee of lamb Therese, boiled potatoes, and a cold buffet including roast beef. None of the cooking was carried out on board. Instead, all the hot and cold food was prepared and cooked in kitchens at the stopover points and placed onboard in vacuum flasks. These were stowed in either the hot box or the ice chest on the aircraft, ready for reheating and serving. After each meal it was the job of the stewards to wash up and stow everything away tidily.

By 1938 Imperial had taken delivery of enough flying boats to extend services through to Singapore, with an aircraft change taking place at Alexandria. At Singapore, Qantas aircraft and crews took over for the onward journey to Sydney. Passengers bound for Hong Kong transferred to a DH.86 landplane at Bangkok. By the end of the year a third weekly service to Durban had been added to the timetable, which now also included seven flights a week to Egypt, four to India, three to South Africa, and two each to Malaya, Hong Kong and Australia. From July 1938 all mail to Australia and New Zealand was also carried unsurcharged under the Empire Air Mail Scheme.

The considerable expansion in traffic made it necessary to schedule dawn take-offs and dusk arrival at Hythe. As naked flames were not permitted on Southampton Water an electric flarepath was developed for use there, and on 24 September 1938 *Canopus* and *Corinthian* became the first flying boats to operate scheduled night departures from Hythe. Along the routes, however, paraffin and kerosene lamps were still being used for flarepaths, with about 150 alighting areas being so equipped. In the meantime much thought was devoted to the establishment of a trans-Tasman air link between

Australia and New Zealand. On 27 December 1937 *Centaurus* arrived at Auckland's Waitemata Harbour on a route-survey flight from Sydney. It was moored alongside the Pan American Airways Sikorsky S.42B flying boat *Samoan Clipper*, which had arrived the previous day on that airline's inaugural service from San Francisco. During its stay the Imperial Airways aircraft paid courtesy visits to Wellington, Lyttelton and Dunedin before setting off back to the UK on 10 January 1938. Press coverage of the visit was favourable but it was soon realised that the C-class machines were not suited to commercial trans-Tasman services, which would have to wait until the introduction of longer-range aircraft.

Imperial Airways was always at pains to ensure that only the most select hotels, managed by Europeans, were used for the overnight accommodation of its passengers. As the route network grew the hotels used included the Grande Bretagne in Rome, the Oriental in Bangkok, and the world-famous Raffles in Singapore. Not all overnight stopovers were in conventional hotels. At Dubai the flying boats alighted on the Dubai Creek, where an extra fee of four rupees was paid by the airline for a nightwatchman to keep an eye on the aircraft while the passengers and crew were taken 10 miles by road to spend the night at Sharjah in a combined fort and hotel complete with steel entrance door, loopholes in the walls for rifles, and an encircling ring of barbed wire. At Crete, while their aircraft was being refuelled, the passengers were taken aboard the Imperial Airways yacht *Imperia* for tea. Houseboats were also used for overnight accommodation, including the *Mayflower* and the *Agamemnon* at Cairo and the *King Richard* at Mozambique. This latter vessel could sleep up to thirty people and had a lounge, dining room, bar and electric lighting. At overnight stops it was customary for the crew to stay in the same accommodation as the passengers, so they all spent a lot of time in each other's company. Some of the hotels in India and the Far East expected their guests to dress formally for dinner, so the crew and passengers needed to remember to pack a dinner jacket or evening dress. During the long flight sectors Imperial provided its passengers with distractions such as playing cards, jigsaw puzzles, crosswords and board games.

Passengers were also issued with annotated route maps, and there was certainly much of interest to be viewed through the promenade deck windows. The leg from Baghdad to Basra routed past the Great Arch of Ctesiphon at Babylon, and on across the areas of marshland between the Tigris and Euphrates rivers. After Iraq the route continued to India, calling at Karachi before night-stopping at Udaipur, where the flying boat alighted on the man-made lake at Rajsamand and a launch took the passengers ashore at the Baripal Dam. The establishment of the landing area here owed much to the support of the Maharana of Udaipur. The facilities there included a station superintendent's office, a meteorological station, a passenger lounge, petrol and oil storage depots, a wireless station, and two residential bungalows. Nearby was a railway station for the 40-mile journey into Udaipur city. The flying boat route then continued onwards to Madho in Gwalior. After this a landing was made on the Parichha reservoir at Jhansi, then a flight onward to Allahabad, followed by a touchdown at the mouth of the River Hooghly at Calcutta. Continuing onwards, the aircraft alighted at Gelugor, about 6 miles from Penang, with the aid of a flarepath of kerosene lamps mounted on 4ft-high floats. These lamps were lit by matches and dropped into position from a fast pinnace travelling along the 1,200-yard alighting area, which also had searchlights stationed at each end. The pinnace carried red Very Light flares that were fired off if an obstruction was spotted on the water. The Imperial aircraft arrived there at around midnight. While it was being refuelled by a Shell launch the local agent, Mansfields, took the passengers ashore for a cup of tea. Departure was at 0300hrs, timed to deliver them in Singapore in time for breakfast. At Singapore the Imperial Airways flying boats made use of the Singapore Marine and Land Airport, which had been officially opened in June 1937. The marine section of the airport had an alighting area a mile long and 600ft wide, enclosed by a boom that kept out floating debris. There were two hangars, a passenger terminal, and a slipway where the C-class machines could be winched ashore for maintenance and repairs.

Occasionally, the flying boat passengers could find themselves making an unscheduled stop. In mid June 1938 *Ceres*, under the command of Captain Gurney, encountered severe weather over India and a precautionary landing was made on Lake Dingari in the state of Tonk, about 50 miles south of Jaipur. In the course of the landing the aircraft ran aground and became stuck on a crocodile-infested mudbank. The crew were unable to contact base by wireless and the nearest telephone was 20 miles away, so someone set off on foot to get help. In the meantime the crew and passengers settled down for the night inside the security of the aircraft, and the stewards prepared dinner before they all tried to get some sleep. Help arrived in the morning and the passengers were transferred by boat to Gwalior, from where they gamely resumed their journey on the next Imperial service. With the aid of a multitude of local helpers, the flying boat was pulled free from the mudbank, but the crew then decided to wait for more favourable winds before attempting a take-off. They finally got airborne on 20 June, having been sustained in the meantime by food and water dropped to them by parachute.

During the autumn of 1938 Short Bros introduced the improved Bristol Perseus-powered S.30 Empire flying boat. Nine examples were built to the order of Imperial Airways, with three of them actually being delivered to Tasman Empire Airways Ltd (TEAL) of New Zealand for operations across the Tasman Sea. As Christmas 1938 drew nearer the mail loads to the Empire increased dramatically. During the third week of December the Imperial fleet flew some 82,000 extra miles on additional services, with passengers being almost completely displaced in favour of heavy mail loads. The loading of the mail was carried out through the night hours in readiness for an early morning departure. When the crew came aboard they found the aircraft interior pre-warmed by an oil heater in the midships compartment, and a breakfast of porridge, bacon and tomato omelettes placed on board in vacuum flasks. All of this extra flying was not accomplished without cost. On 27 November 1938 *Calpurnia* was operating a Christmas mail service without passengers and the crew were preparing to alight at Habbaniyah, about 25 miles west of Baghdad, when they encountered a dust storm and hit the sea heavily. All the crew were lost and the aircraft was destroyed.

The passing of the Southampton Harbour Act of 1939 confirmed the city's status as a major flying boat terminus and gave the Southampton Harbour Board powers to regulate the use of seaplanes and flying boats there, with a 'reserved area' being established off Netley.

On 14 March 1939 *Corsair* had to make a forced landing in the Belgian Congo, and so began a marathon salvage operation to recover it. The aircraft was operating a northbound service on the African route, and had taken off from Port Bell, Uganda, for Juba, some 350 miles away. Problems with the flying boat's direction-finding equipment had been reported by the crews of previous services, but the fault had supposedly been rectified. The flight's route should have taken *Corsair* along the path of the Nile until Juba was reached, but by the estimated time of arrival there the crew had still not seen any sign of the river. For two hours they flew around with no idea of their location until they only had enough fuel for another fifteen minutes and were then forced to alight on a waterway that turned out to be the River Dungu, near to a town called Faradje. During the landing the flying boat sustained damage to its hull and the crew ran it ashore on the riverbank.

In due course the local provincial commissioner arrived at the scene and took charge of the thirteen passengers, the luggage and the mail, driving them initially to his house, then to a small hotel about 50 miles away, and eventually to Juba. A couple of days later *Centurion* arrived there on the next northbound schedule and took them home to Hythe. When Imperial Airways heard about the incident they contacted Short Bros, who sent a team of engineers out to the scene to assess the damage. They reported that the bottom of the hull had been torn out and initially estimated that it would take about six weeks to get the aircraft airworthy again. However, they would later revise this estimate to three months. Imperial Airways was already short of C-class machines, having lost several in accidents. The Second World War was looming, and Short Bros was heavily committed to priority production of Sunderland flying boats for the RAF, so the construction of a replacement aircraft would take a long time. Imperial needed to get *Corsair* back into service, so work began on the laborious on-site repair work. A slipway was built using local labour and the aircraft was hauled up onto the riverbank by May. The work was eventually completed and the flying boat was hauled back onto the water and made ready for flight. Early on the morning of 14 July the crew attempted a take-off, but the flying boat swung fiercely to starboard and the float on that side made contact with the riverbank. The engines were cut, but the nose swung into the bank, the hull struck a rock, and a new 11ft gash appeared. Imperial despatched a party of its own engineers to assist those already at the scene, but shortly afterwards war was declared and the Short Bros workforce was recalled to the UK, leaving the Imperial staff to carry on with the work, assisted by local labour. They designed and constructed a crude device for working underwater and with the aid of this they were able to attach a metal patch over the damaged portion of the hull and pump the water out. On 5 October 1939 they were able to get a message to head office advising that *Corsair* was again watertight. They then floated it across the river and hauled it up onto the slipway while they dammed the river downstream to raise the water level and make a second take-off attempt more likely to succeed. While this work was in progress Christmas came, and Imperial in London sent out half a dozen hampers containing seasonal fare so the work party could celebrate in the traditional manner. By the end of 1939 the dam was complete and the flying boat was hauled back onto the water. Imperial head office decreed that such a hazardous take-off should be entrusted to one of its most experienced pilots, and Captain Jack Kelly-Rogers was despatched to the site. Early on the morning of 6 January 1940 he successfully lifted *Corsair* off the river and flew it to Alexandria for a full overhaul and eventual return to service.

On 6 June 1939 Imperial Airways had opened its new Airways House headquarters in London's Buckingham Palace Road. At that time this was the only building of its size devoted entirely to air travel, and contained, among other passenger facilities, a buffet and a women passengers' retiring room. From that date the connecting train services to Southampton switched their departure point from Waterloo to Imperial's private Platform 17 at Victoria Station, adjacent to the new terminal building. Imperial's passengers departed Victoria at 2005hrs, with dinner being served on the train en route. During that year the twin pontoons at Southampton were used for eight flight arrivals and eight departures each week. In the summer of 1939 an article by one of the airline's commanders appeared in the *Imperial Airways Gazette*. Titled 'We Leave At Dawn', it described in detail the procedures involved in operating the first leg of an Australia service, from Southampton to Marseilles:

> Looking out of the window at 3am one is pleasantly surprised to see no trace of the wind and rain that was blustering outside overnight … Stars are out and the night is clear. We are the third 'boat' away this morning. 'Corialanus' is already well over the Channel, and 'Carpentaria' is just now leaving the raft (pontoon), cabin windows alight, a red glow on the port wingtip as it turns south soon replaced by the white tail light as it makes its way down the buoyed channel. The crane is loading mails fast into our own craft 'Canopus' while the engineers who start up the engines this morning and the traffic staff are in and out of the narrow beam of light from the lower forward hold and the control cabin above … The First Officer is already aboard and has checked the fuel carried, the equipment and maps, the drift sight and log books, also primed the exactor mixture and throttle controls (if not already done by the engineers), the proper lighting of the cockpit and instruments, plugged in the Aldis Lamp, and tried the flap motor. The Radio Officer has tested receiver and transmitter and is now below at the bow-hatch wearing his electric torch strapped around his head to leave his hands free. While the steward sees the last of the passengers to their seats and explains that the sound of the flap motor and the flames that will come out of the engine exhausts are perfectly normal happenings the Flight Clerk fastens each hatch in turn and reports when the last of the engineers has left the machine. On receipt of the 'all-clear for starting' the flying-boat is

warped forward ten or fifteen feet and the engines started … The tail line is released from the control cabin and immediately the 'Sydney Eastbound' service eases forward out of the raft under its own power. It joins the ebb tide down the fairway and becomes a member of the fraternity of shipping which use this waterway … a launch goes ahead, on watch for obstructions … No. 2 launch has taken up station at the far end of the flarepath, and a steady white light in answer to our Aldis signal 'OKTO' gives us permission to take off and affirms the area has been found clear of flotsam … A final check is made, then the engines are opened up fully and the flying-boat is rapidly up on its 'step' and into its proper medium … As we square away onto course the trip-clock is started. The Shell wharves and Calshot are soon left to starboard, Hamble and Lee-on-Solent and Gosport to port. All of these are left behind and in under six minutes 'Canopus' is over the Isle of Wight.

The romantic aura of flying boat travel captured the imagination of the public, and versions of the plastic scale models displayed in the windows of travel agencies were produced for sale in toyshops, in kit form for 15s or fully assembled for 52s 6d.

The Imperial Airways timetable for April 1939 included twice-weekly services to South Africa, with a once-weekly stop at Lake Naivasha in Kenya's Great Rift Valley, subject to 'circumstances permitting and inducement offered'. However, the C-class flying boats had proven to be vulnerable to damage on the demanding routes they operated, and by mid 1939, within two years of the first delivery, nine examples had been written off in accidents. In the summer of 1939 Major Mayo, the Technical Advisor to Imperial Airways, summarised in a lecture some of the type's other shortfalls. Paraphrased, these were:

- The type was deficient in payload, mainly because of the way it was operated. Although carrying only a small number of passengers, its performance was impaired by the substantial weight of luxurious fittings and plush furnishings it had to carry.
- The original timetables had been based on the performance of landplanes, but the lack of night-flying aids and inadequate weather forecasting facilities meant that hardly any night flying was scheduled, making overall journey times far longer than anticipated.

- Costings had been based on the assumption that fuel prices at coastal or waterway locations would be lower than those at land airports. To some extent this might have been so, but the expense of establishing water-borne refuelling points far outweighed any fuel price savings.
- The aircraft's engines had a short service life. Many of the staging posts along the routes had no facilities for beaching aircraft, so engine changes had to be carried out on the water. If the conditions were too rough the engineers had to wait for better weather before they could proceed.

Designs for improved flying boats were under development, but before they could be produced and the other issues addressed the Second World War intervened.

# 2

# PAN AMERICAN ACROSS THE PACIFIC

In the USA at the beginning of the 1930s Pan American Airways was starting to establish a route system to Latin America and South America using flying boats. The airline's founder, Juan Trippe, was trying to attract passengers who normally patronised the ocean liners, and in 1931 he registered the trademark name Clipper for use on his aircraft and publicity literature to convey some of the aura and heritage of the clipper sailing ships. The first Pan American marine aircraft to carry the Clipper branding was the Sikorsky S-40. This was not a pure flying boat as it also had a wheeled undercarriage for land operations. It was powered by four Pratt & Whitney Hornet piston engines and was capable of carrying up to forty passengers seated four-abreast in railway-style compartments. The chairs were fashioned in Queen Anne style and upholstered in blue and orange, and the floor of the passenger accommodation was covered in blue carpeting. A smoking lounge was provided, and to further while away the time the passengers had access to playing cards, jigsaw puzzles, and chess and backgammon sets. In the lounge, life preservers were prominently attached to the walls. Pan American's three S-40s, named *America Clipper*, *Caribbean Clipper* and *Southern Clipper*, entered service in 1931 and operated successfully to Santiago (Chile), Buenos Aires, Rio de Janeiro, Bogota and Lima, but the type was not equipped for night flying and lacked the range to operate across the Pacific Ocean to Asia. Pan American issued a specification for a modern long-range oceanic flying boat and invited tenders from the major aircraft manufacturers. The Sikorsky company responded with its S-42 design. This featured a full-length, two-step, all-metal hull with a strut-braced wing

A Pan American Airways Sikorsky S-42 in flight over Miami. (Pan American Historical Foundation)

mounted above it on a shallow superstructure. Wire-braced wingtip floats were carried on two struts, and a structure on the rear of the hull supported a semi-braced tailplane, above which were mounted twin fins and rudders. The aircraft was to be powered by four 700hp Pratt & Whitney Hornet piston engines bestowing a cruising speed of 150–160mph and a cruising range of 1,200 miles, reduced to 750 miles if a full payload was carried. It would be crewed by two pilots, an engineer, a radio operator and a steward, and the price fully equipped was quoted as US$242,000. Pan American viewed the aircraft as the next logical step for the expansion of its flying boat services, and placed an order for three examples on 1 October 1932. The S-42 made its maiden flight on 30 March 1934, and on 1 August that year Pan American conducted its own evaluation flight, with a crew that included the airline's chief test pilot, Captain Edwin Musick, and its technical advisor, the renowned transatlantic aviator Charles Lindbergh, taking it around a 1,242-mile course with a representative load of thirty-two passengers plus cargo and mail. On 16 August 1934 the S-42 entered Pan American service from Miami to Buenos Aires and Rio de Janeiro, cutting the travel time from eight days to five. On arrival in Rio the S-42, registered NC822M, was named *Brazilian Clipper* by the wife of the Brazilian president. The three original S-42s were later joined by four improved S-42As, and also from 1937 by three twenty-four-seat S-42Bs, and the family of aircraft saw extensive service on routes to the Caribbean, Latin America and South America.

Boarding the S-42 was accomplished via a short 'Jacob's Ladder' over the side and across the rubber-covered walkways, formed by open hatch covers being laid back onto the deck. Upon entering the cabin area the passengers would have been impressed by the aircraft's yacht-like proportions. The passenger accommodation was divided into four compartments, each containing eight seats. All of these were adjustable, and were suspended from the bulkheads. The lack of chair legs reaching down to the floor meant there could be more under-seat storage space. The walls and ceiling of this compartment were lined with walnut veneer panels, and pads of rubber and horsehair between these panels and the bulkheads dampened down vibration and helped with soundproofing. Since the S-42s were intended for operation in tropical climates only, no heating system was installed. The second compartment was twice the size of the others and had the general appearance of a large lounge. Immediately behind the passenger compartments were toilets and also storage areas that could be converted to accommodate sleeper berths. These operated on the same principle as Pullman railway compartments. Dressing and undressing could be carried out in privacy in the large lounge-like compartment, behind a special divider curtain that was erected each night and morning. Ingenious fold-out washbasins with hot and cold running water made the lounge compartment an adequate dressing room. At the front of the aircraft a door in the forward cockpit bulkhead allowed the crew access to the anchor winch and to a hatchway in the deck.

Plans had been proposed for the licensed production of S-42As in the UK by British Marine Aircraft, and ground was cleared at Hamble for this, but the scheme was not carried through. Pan American had originally envisaged its S-42s being utilised on services to Europe, but by the time all three examples had been delivered in mid 1934 permission for transatlantic scheduled flights had still not been granted due to political and diplomatic delays. The airline needed to start earning revenue with these expensive machines, and so for the time being it turned its sights to the Pacific Ocean. However, despite their successful operation on Caribbean and South American services where the longest sector scheduled was under 600 miles, it soon became apparent that the S-42 family of aircraft did not have the range for the critical 2,400-mile stage between San Francisco and Honolulu on Pacific routes. The airline had already placed an order for the new Martin M-130 flying boat, which would be capable of covering the distance, but deliveries were a year behind schedule. As route survey flights would need to be carried out before scheduled services could begin, in the spring of 1935 the second S-42, NC823M, was stripped of all passenger fittings and fitted with extra fuel tanks in the main cabin. On 16 April 1935 it set off from San Francisco for Honolulu. After safely arriving there it was then used for survey flights between Honolulu and Pan American's Pacific island staging posts. On 17 March 1937 the S-42B NC16734 *Clipper III*, under the command of Captain Edwin Musick, took off from the Alameda Naval Air Station at San Francisco for a survey flight to Auckland, New Zealand via Honolulu, Kingman Reef (a tiny island 1,100 miles south of Honolulu), and Pago Pago in American Samoa. The leg from Alameda to Honolulu took nineteen hours fifteen minutes, and after the second leg there was a five-day stopover at Kingman Reef, where a merchant ship anchored in the lagoon was used to provide a sheltered mooring place for the flying boat. After Pago Pago was reached a hurricane in the vicinity forced another five-day stopover before the crew of seven could set off on the final leg to Auckland. Here, the aircraft's arrival at Waitemata Harbour on 29 March was witnessed by around 3,000 New Zealanders lining the waterfront. The crew attended formal receptions and took local dignitaries on a two-hour sightseeing flight before they departed on the return journey on 4 April. On 11 January 1938 Captain Musick was back at Pago Pago with the S-42B NC16734, now renamed *Samoan Clipper*, and a new crew on further route survey duties. That day they were to carry out a final check flight before scheduled airmail services between the USA and New Zealand were inaugurated. An hour or so after take-off a radio message was sent, advising that they had developed engine problems and would be returning to Pago Pago after dumping fuel to lighten the aircraft for landing. Nothing more was heard from them, and the aircraft was not sighted again. An investigation into the disappearance concluded that fuel vapours must have ignited during the dumping procedure and caused an explosion as the crew were attempting an emergency landing on the sea. In spite of this disaster the remaining S-42Bs remained in Pan American service. The *Bermuda Clipper* was transferred to Manila to provide connecting flights from there to Hong Kong, and four examples of the S-42 family were to survive the Second World War, not being scrapped until mid 1946.

Before scheduled services across the Pacific could be inaugurated Pan American had to locate suitable points at which its aircraft could stop over on the long journey between the Midway Island and the US island dependency of Guam, and construct high-standard accommodation for its passengers. The airline's investigations revealed the existence of a small uninhabited coral island called Wake, handily located 1,260 miles from Midway and 1,560 miles from Guam. Before Wake could be used, however, it was necessary to use explosives to blast a channel through the surrounding reef and provide a passage to the lagoon where the flying boats could be moored safely. None of the island stopping points on the route to Manila had weather forecasting facilities or any of the other equipment needed to look after passengers during stopovers, so in early 1935 Pan American leased the cargo ship *North Haven* to convey all the supplies and manpower needed to build a chain of flying boat bases across the Pacific. On her first voyage the ship carried prefabricated hotels and support buildings, construction equipment, a four-month supply of food, 250 gallons of aviation fuel, and around 120 personnel, including demolition experts, labourers and other workers. The *North Haven* then made a second trip with items for furnishing the stopover hotels, including bed linen, bridge tables, terrace furniture, and beach umbrellas. It was Juan Trippe's ambition to provide idyllic stays for his passengers. Each of the hotels had twenty-four double bedrooms with electric lighting and showers. Tons of rich soil were shipped in to provide a fertile base for the lawns and gardens. The hotel at Wake was actually sited on nearby Peale Island. From its veranda guests would be able to look out across the lagoon and witness the surf crashing onto the coral reef. Launches were to be made available for deep-sea fishing trips. The task of constructing the chain of bases on the islands was completed in only fifty-five days. The trans-Pacific routeing was finalised as San Francisco–Honolulu–Midway–Wake–Guam–Manila. The first flying boat to pass through Wake arrived on 17 August 1935 en route to Canton Island, an atoll some 1,900 miles south-west of Hawaii.

In the meantime, the Martin M-130 flying boat had made its maiden flight on 30 December 1934. The design had been submitted to Pan American in competition with the Sikorsky S-42 in the early 1930s, and the airline had placed an order for three examples at a unit price of US$417,200 each fully equipped, more than double the cost of the S-42. Production delays meant that Pan American did not take delivery of its first M-130 until 9 October 1935, over a year behind schedule. It was a larger

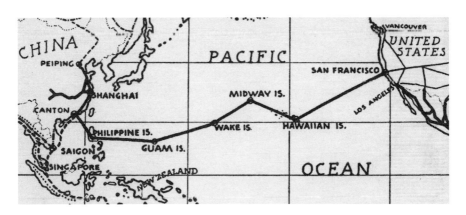

A diagram of Pan American's flying-boat route across the Pacific to the Far East. (via author)

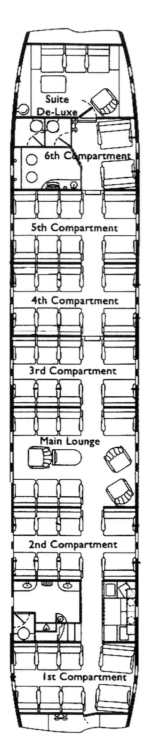

aircraft than the S-42, was of strut-braced metal construction, and had a single fin and rudder unit. Instead of wing-tip floats, stability on the water was enhanced by large hull sponsons that also acted as fuel tanks. Power was provided by four 830hp (later increased to 950hp) Pratt & Whitney Twin Wasp piston engines, conferring a cruising speed of 157mph. The range varied from 4,000 miles with mail only or 3,200 miles with mail plus passengers. The maximum capacity was forty-one daytime passengers or thirty on overnight flights, but the requirement to carry sufficient fuel for the critical San Francisco–Honolulu sector usually meant that only eight to fourteen passengers could be carried on this leg, depending on forecast winds. The M-130's interior included a large lounge compartment for twelve people that could be converted for overnight use into sleeping berth accommodation. Folding washbasins with hot and cold running water were also fitted in the lounge area, and the aircraft also incorporated two smaller passenger compartments. All the fittings were designed to be rapidly removable to reduce weight if necessary. As the aircraft was unpressurised it was possible to open any of the ten large passenger windows to obtain better views of the passing scenery. The interior décor was the creation of Norman Bel Geddes, a former New York City theatre set designer and part of the art deco movement. As well as selecting the upholstery and fittings for the

Diagram of seating layout on Pan American Boeing 314s. (via author)

A Pan American Boeing 314 dwarfs the crew members around it. (via author)

passenger areas, he also had a hand in the design of the aircraft's crockery, providing the plates and saucers with a vacuum base that allowed them to remain in place during rough weather.

On 22 November 1935 the Martin M-130 NC14716 *China Clipper* inaugurated the world's first regular trans-Pacific air service, from Alameda Naval Air Station at San Francisco to Manila via Honolulu, Midway, Wake and Guam. At first the service was restricted to the carriage of mail, but in September 1936, after many flights had been successfully completed and the US Department of Commerce had completed an exhaustive investigation of the facilities and equipment at the stopover points, approval was given for the carriage of fare-paying passengers. The fare through to Manila was high. When inflation is taken into account it was twice as expensive per passenger

The interior of Pan American's Dinner Key terminal at Miami in 1934. (Pan American Historical Foundation)

mile as the supersonic Concorde of the 1970s, but it was a price the well-heeled were prepared to pay, the first ticket for the service being issued to R.F. Bradley, the aviation manager of Standard Oil.

On 21 October 1936 the inaugural passenger service was operated by NC14714 *Hawaiian Clipper* under the command of the ill-fated Captain Edwin Musick. On board were five male and two female passengers plus a relief crew. As soon as cruising altitude was reached the two stewards served a luncheon buffet. Later on there was 'cocktail hour' to look forward to. Then came dinner. Among the items on the menu was grilled filet mignon, which had been placed aboard the aircraft 90 per cent cooked and then frozen, ready for finishing off in the oven. At midnight those passengers still awake and hungry were offered a supper of sandwiches, cold cuts and salad, with milk or hot chocolate, before turning in for the night. Pan American's Pacific Division employed sixteen stewards who had all completed six months of training at the airline's facility at Treasure Island, San Francisco. The curriculum there included training on how to survive on an uninhabited island after an emergency landing. The stewards were routinely responsible for purchasing all the ingredients for the meals to be served along the route, including fresh meat, vegetables and eggs. After the overnight flight from San Francisco the passengers were woken by the stewards in time to dress and have a cup of coffee before enjoying the views of the Hawaiian islands passing by below. As they came ashore at Honolulu they were greeted by hula dancing girls and presented with the traditional Hawaiian leis before enjoying a twenty-four-hour stopover. Despite having to battle against headwinds and circumnavigate storms, the inaugural service arrived safely at Manila on 27 October. From here, onward connections to Hong Kong by S-42 flying boats were available. As fate would have it, all three of the Pan American M-130s were to be destroyed in accidents in later years. On 29 July 1938 the *Hawaiian Clipper*, with six passengers and nine crew aboard, disappeared without trace between Guam and Manila. The *Philippine Clipper* struck a mountain about 100 miles north of San Francisco on 21 January 1943, and the *China Clipper* sank during an attempted night landing at Port of Spain, Trinidad, on 8 January 1945.

As well as providing comfortable accommodation for its passengers at the island stopover points, Pan American also needed to construct impressive terminals befitting a world-class airline on the US mainland, and much

The sleeping berth arrangement aboard a Pan American Airways Martin M-130 on the trans-Pacific routes. (via author)

effort went into making these as prestigious as possible. The main flying boat base was to be at Dinner Key, in the Coconut Grove area of Miami. The first ground was broken here on 22 February 1931 and the completed terminal was dedicated on 25 March 1934. Although landing facilities for landplanes were also provided, the base was intended primarily for flying boats and was designed to be capable of handling up to four Clippers simultaneously. Covered walkways protected passengers from the weather as they boarded or disembarked, and the terminal also had outdoor verandas on both floors, where spectators could watch the aircraft movements in comfort and try to spot celebrities passing through. These spectator areas were to become a popular feature of Pan American terminals elsewhere. The interior of the first floor of the Dinner Key terminal was dominated by a giant world globe, 10ft in diameter and powered by an electric motor that caused it to rotate completely every two minutes. On its surface were displayed the routeing and destination of every airborne Pan American service. Electrically operated bulletin boards kept passengers and others updated on all arrivals and departures. On the second floor a dining room with seating for 100 overlooked Biscayne Bay.

The actual boarding of a flight was to develop into something of a ritual, controlled by the port manager from his office by means of bell signals. At the first signal the crew embarked. When the departing passengers received the signal to board they proceeded down to the lower level and along one of the covered walkways to the appropriate boarding float and on to the aircraft. Arriving passengers were directed upstairs, firstly to the premises of the US Public Health Service, and then to the customs and immigration examination rooms. Dinner Key was to continue to serve Pan American until the final departure from there on 9 August 1945. In 1952 the site was sold to the City of Miami for US$1 million and the former terminal became part of Miami City Hall.

In 1935 the Pan American terminal in San Francisco was located just south of the new bridge spanning the bay between San Francisco and Oakland, at the former Curtiss-Wright airfield. In 1938 the City of San Francisco and Pan American jointly proposed to the US government that San Francisco should host a Golden Gate Exhibition in 1939. Included in the proposal was the relocation of Pan American's flying boat terminal to Treasure Island, an area of some 400 acres of reclaimed land in the middle of San Francisco Bay. The proposal was approved, and a twenty-year lease on the land was signed in August 1938. On 5 February 1939 the opening of Pan American's new flying boat terminal was marked by the departure from there of the *China Clipper*. Thirteen days later the Golden Gate International Exposition opened. One of the major draws was a visit to the new flying boat terminal, now called the 'Port of the Trade Winds'. This comprised three permanent buildings, with two of them being used for the maintenance and housing of the aircraft. For the duration of the Exposition the public could view this work in progress from a gallery viewpoint located in the Hall of Air Transportation. The area of water adjacent to the hangars was named Clipper Cove. In the event of adverse weather in the San Francisco area Pan American could use a designated alternative alighting area at Clear Lake, California.

In March 1939 the airline entered into an agreement with the City of New York for the lease of land for a new flying boat base at the existing La Guardia landplane airport. In due course a hangar and a new terminal building known as the Marine Air Terminal were constructed at a cost of US$40 million. The facility was just to the north of the site for the 1939–40 New York World's Fair. On its completion Pan American transferred its flying boat services across from its previous base at Port Washington. On 31 March 1940 the new terminal was dedicated as the new home of the airline's North Atlantic Clipper services, and on that same day it gained the status of an international airport when the *Yankee Clipper* lifted off from the waters of the Rikers Island Channel on its way to Lisbon.

During their flight testing and service life the Martin M-130s established some nineteen aviation records, but as early as October 1936 the *San Francisco Chronicle* was announcing details released by the Boeing company of the fleet of six gigantic double-deck flying boats under construction for Pan American to supercede them. The Boeing 314s would be of all-metal light alloy stressed skin construction and would be powered by four of the most powerful engines then available, the 1,500hp Wright Cyclone GR-2600. The powerplants would be mounted on a high wing, and the aircraft would have a single fin and rudder unit. Protruding from each side of the lower part of the hull would be two-spar sponsons called 'seawings', which would aid stability on the water and also house fuel that could be pumped up to the wing tanks. The wing itself would have a cavernous interior, thick enough to permit an engineer to access and adjust the engines in flight by means of an internal walkway. The operating crew would consist of a

A Pan American Airways Martin M-130 moored at the terminal at Dinner Key, Miami. (Florida Memory Store)

captain, first officer, navigator/second officer, engineer, and radio officer, and in service a complete relief crew would be carried. The flight deck would be on the upper deck, which would also contain an area for the stowage of charts and technical manuals, and bunks for the off-duty crew members. All the passenger accommodation would be on the lower deck. The contract for six aircraft at a cost of US$550,000 each had been signed on 21 July 1936. On 7 June 1938 the Boeing 314 made its maiden flight. Initial problems with flight stability were remedied by the addition of two more fins and rudders to the tail assembly, and Pan American's first aircraft was handed over on 27 January 1939. The rest of the aircraft followed during that year, and they were speedily placed into service on the airline's Pacific route network.

Boeing had originally designed the 314 to accommodate seventy-four seated passengers or forty in sleeper berths, but in Pan American service the sleeper capacity was to be reduced to thirty-four. The passenger accommodation was divided up into compartments called 'staterooms', each of which seated ten people during the day. At night the stewards converted each stateroom into an overnight sleeper compartment containing six berths. This procedure was similar to that carried out in Pullman railway carriages, and took almost thirty minutes to complete. Full-length privacy curtains in 'Pan American Blue' protected the passengers' modesty. The social gathering spot on board was the lounge, which seated eleven people and could be transformed into a dining room at mealtimes. Before dinner was served the passengers could enjoy cocktails in their staterooms, where little tables could be pulled out to hold their glasses and hors d'oeuvres. The ladies' powder room was decorated in art deco style and furnished with a dressing table, two leather-covered swivel stools and a mirror. A washbasin supplied hot and cold running water. At the very rear of the passenger compartments was a private suite, sometimes called the Bridal Suite. This contained a three-cushion 'Davenport' that converted into upper and lower berths, black walnut side tables with shelves for magazines, a small 'love-seat', a coffee table, a wardrobe, a small dressing table, and a concealed washbasin.

In July 1938 Boeing released a sketch of the interior layout of a proposed successor to the 314. This would have resembled a scaled-up version of its predecessor, but with retractable wing-floats and a hull of improved aerodynamic profile. Power would have been provided by six engines built into the wing. In the event, the proposal was not proceeded with. After a series of route-proving flights the Pan American Boeing 314 NC18606 *American Clipper* inaugurated a twice-monthly service between San Francisco and Auckland via Honolulu, Canton Island, and Noumea in New Caledonia on 12 July 1940, arriving in New Zealand six days later. From 16 September that year the service connected at Auckland with the TEAL Empire flying boat service to Sydney. During October 1941 the Pan American flights between Honolulu and Auckland also included a stop at Suva in Fiji, but following the Japanese attack on Pearl Harbor, Hawaii, on 7 December 1941 the airline suspended its Pacific routes, and Pan American flying boats were not to be seen again at Auckland until June 1946.

# 3

# TRANSATLANTIC BEGINNINGS

At the start of the 1930s the ambitions of the airlines of operating regular services linking North America and Europe remained unattainable as the contemporary airliners lacked the range to tackle the vast distances across the North Atlantic. Until more capable aircraft could be introduced Pan American Airways decided to devote its energies to opening air services between New York and the British colonial island of Bermuda, and managed to persuade Imperial Airways to co-operate on a joint operation. In 1934 the British government and the Bermudan authorities granted permission for mail and passenger services on the route. This was followed in 1935 by an agreement between the two airlines not to compete directly on this route or on future services between the UK and New York. This became known as the 'Gentlemen's Agreement', and specified that each airline would operate two round trips between London and New York each week when this became possible. Until then, preparations went ahead for the more modest New York–Bermuda service.

On 12 June 1937 a flying boat base was opened at Darrell's Island, close to Hamilton, Bermuda. The location had been selected because of the sheltered nature of the surrounding stretches of water, and the base incorporated a hangar large enough to house the flying boats of Pan American and Imperial. As befitted an island playground of the rich and famous, the terminal building was luxurious, with lounges, showers and a restaurant. Imperial Airways planned to allocate two Empire flying boats, *Centaurus* and *Cavalier* to the route, and fitted them with additional fuel tanks in the wings to increase their still-air range to 1,078 nautical miles. However, the airline's management was under great pressure to allocate more flying boats

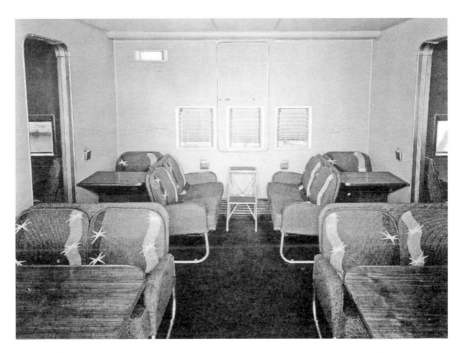

One of the passenger compartments in a Pan American Boeing 314. (Pan American Historical Foundation)

to the Empire and Mediterranean routes, and was forced to announce that only *Cavalier* could be spared for the Bermuda service. This aircraft was not flown out to Bermuda, instead being dismantled and despatched by sea inside twenty-one crates. It arrived safely, was re-assembled, and made a test flight on 19 February 1937. By mid June of that year both airlines had completed their proving flights over the route and were ready to commence scheduled services. Imperial Airways inaugurated its services on the morning of 16 June, when *Cavalier* flew from Bermuda to Port Washington, New York, with fourteen passengers. The aircraft alighted at New York thirty minutes behind schedule as its captain had taken his passengers for a sightseeing detour over the city before landing. The distance of around 700 miles had been covered in a little over six hours, and throughout the flight messages from the flightdeck were broadcast to the public over their wireless sets. That evening, the aircraft's commander, Captain Cumming, was the guest of honour at a dinner hosted by Pan American in the Cloud Room of the Chrysler Building.

Pan American inaugurated its own services on 18 June when its Sikorsky S-42B NC16735 *Bermuda Clipper* transported twenty-eight passengers from New York to Bermuda. It had been agreed that each airline would initially operate one round trip each week, increasing to twice-weekly from August or September. As the Port Washington base at New York was prone to becoming ice-bound from November to March, the US mainland terminal point would be transferred to Baltimore during the winter months. Many celebrities were carried by both carriers, who tried various innovations to attract well-heeled clientele to their services. On Thanksgiving Day in November 1938 Imperial Airways served a traditional Thanksgiving dinner of turkey with cranberry sauce to its passengers en route to Bermuda. However, the airline's Bermuda service came to an abrupt end on 21 January 1939. *Cavalier*, with eight passengers and five crew aboard, developed engine trouble on its way to the island and had to force-land on the sea. The aircraft was evacuated and broke up after fifteen minutes in the heavy swell. Sadly, three of the occupants perished before a rescue ship picked up the survivors. A replacement aircraft could not be spared, and Imperial withdrew from the route, leaving Pan American to maintain services on its own and to eventually introduce larger Boeing 314 equipment.

A Pan American Boeing 314 is made secure after its arrival at Southampton. (via author)

During 1937 Pan American had used Sikorsky S-42B NC16736 *Clipper III* for several route survey flights out of New York in preparation for the eventual opening of scheduled services across the North Atlantic to Europe. Each flight ventured a little further towards Europe. The first one went as far as Shediac in New Brunswick, Canada, and the second one to Botswood, Newfoundland, again in Canada. On 5 July *Clipper III* flew from New York to Botwood via Shediac, and stayed overnight before continuing onward to Foynes in Ireland and finally to Southampton, where it arrived on 8 July and stayed for almost a week. The final survey flight was over a southerly routeing, to Southampton via Lisbon and Marseilles.

Imperial Airways was also conducting trials of its own, in the opposite direction. Although it had been accepted that the C-class flying boats were impractical for scheduled transatlantic service, it was felt that they could provide valuable operating experience if two of them were stripped of all passenger facilities and fitted with extra fuel tanks. Thus modified, *Caledonia* was flown across to Botwood via Foynes on 5 July 1937, later continuing onward to Montreal and New York. In July 1938 Imperial trialled a more unusual method of achieving the necessary range for flights across the Atlantic. A small four-engined seaplane named *Mercury* was mounted on top of a modified Empire flying boat called *Maia*, and on 21 July this two-aircraft combination lifted off from the River Shannon in Ireland using the power of all eight engines of both machines. At a pre-determined altitude the locking device holding *Mercury* in position was released and the seaplane successfully flew on to Montreal with a payload of around 1,000lb of mail and newsreel films. After alighting there twenty hours later the aircraft was refuelled and later flew on to Port Washington, New York, arriving to a tremendous reception from the waiting crowds. A few days later, taking advantage of the favourable prevailing winds, *Mercury* took off under its own power and flew back to the UK via Botwood, the Azores, and Lisbon. Imperial harboured hopes of gaining Air Ministry support for the construction of ten more such combinations for transatlantic and Empire route mail services, but this was not forthcoming.

Another experiment aimed at giving the Imperial Airways flying boats transatlantic range took place during 1939, this time involving air-to-air refuelling. Two C-class machines, *Cabot* and *Caribou*, were used, supported by several Handley Page Harrow transport aircraft that Sir Alan Cobham's Flight Refuelling Ltd had acquired and converted into tankers. One Harrow was based at Shannon in Ireland, and two more at Hattie's Camp (later to

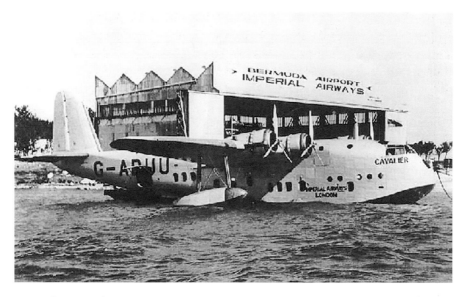

Imperial Airways Short S.23 G-ADUU *Cavalier* at the Darrell's Island flying-boat base on Bermuda. (via author)

be renamed Gander Airport) in Newfoundland. During the trials, which were usually conducted at an altitude of 1,000ft, the Harrow tanker aircraft transferred by hose 800 gallons of fuel to the flying boat in the space of around twelve minutes. Fifteen successful fuel transfers were accomplished over the Atlantic before the trials were terminated.

In late 1937 Imperial Airways had been in discussions with Short Bros regarding the possibility of producing a development of the C–class flying boat fitted with the powerful new 1,380hp Bristol Hercules IV engines. The proposed S.26 aircraft would be larger and heavier than the C class, with a cruising speed of around 180mph and twice the range, enough for transatlantic service. An order for three examples, to be known as the G class in Imperial Airways service, was duly placed and the first example, G-AFCI *Golden Hind*, made its maiden flight on 21 July 1939. It was handed over to the airline for crew training on 24 September that year, but before it could enter passenger service the Second World War intervened and all three examples built were transferred to the RAF.

This was also the year in which Pan American Airways was able to make serious progress with its plans for services to Europe, having taken delivery of a suitable aircraft, the Boeing 314. On 23 February the first example to be allocated to the airline's Atlantic Division, NC18603, was ferried from San Francisco to its new base, the Marine Terminal at Baltimore's Logan Airport. On 3 March it was flown to Anacosta, Maryland, where the First Lady Eleanor Roosevelt christened it *Atlantic Clipper* using a bottle filled with water from the 'seven seas'. After completing a route survey flight around Europe the same aircraft inaugurated a scheduled mail service from Port Washington, New York, to Marseilles over the southern routeing via the Azores and Lisbon on 20 March, and also inaugurated mail services over the northern routeing to Southampton via Shediac, Botwood and Foynes on 24 June. Under the terms of its operating licence Pan American was required to successfully complete five mail-only round trips across the Atlantic before it could be permitted to carry fare-paying passengers. Once passenger-carrying services began these would be restricted to two landings in Europe each week. After completing the specified number of mail services, Pan American opened regular passenger services on 28 June 1939 when NC18605 *Dixie Clipper*, under the command of Captain R.O.D. Sullivan, carried twenty-two passengers to Southampton on the southern routeing via Horta in the Azores, Lisbon and Marseilles. Passenger services over the northern routeing were inaugurated by the *Yankee Clipper* carrying seventeen passengers, and these two Boeing 314s were later joined on the North Atlantic run by NC18606 *American Clipper*.

Pan American Airways Sikorsky S-42B NC16736 during a visit to Hythe, near Southampton. (via author)

Departures from the small floating dock at the Marine Air Terminal at La Guardia, New York were complicated by the fact that, once they had boarded, the passengers would only be able to use one of the doors to exit in the event of an engine fire during start-up. Therefore, as a precaution, a routine was introduced whereby the two flight engineers would board the Boeing first, and would be running through their checklists by the time the rest of the crew smartly marched aboard. Only once all four engines were running satisfactorily would the passengers be permitted to board. At the other end of the journey, the pontoons at Berth 108 at Southampton could not at that time accommodate aircraft as large as the Boeing 314, and so the passengers and crew had to be transported out to their Clipper by motor launch. With the outbreak of the Second World War the northern routeing across the Atlantic was suspended, but Pan American's Boeings continued to maintain transatlantic services over a South Atlantic routeing via Brazil and West Africa. Pan American's last Boeing 314, NC18602 *California Clipper*, was not retired by the airline until 1946.

# 4

# WARTIME INTERLUDE

The wartime efforts of Pan American Airways and Imperial Airways (which on 1 April 1940 was merged with the pre-war British Airways to form the British Overseas Airways Corporation, usually shortened to BOAC) to maintain some sort of passenger and mail service under trying wartime conditions would fill several books, so what follows is a brief résumé of their flying boat activities.

Upon the declaration of war in 1939 the Imperial Airways base at Southampton was considered to be vulnerable to air attack in view of the proximity of the nearby docks and Supermarine aircraft factory, and the flying boat services were transferred to a more remote location at Poole in Dorset, although the servicing facilities were to remain at nearby Hythe throughout the war. The absence of bombing raids during the so-called 'Phoney War' period lulled the authorities into a false sense of security, and the flying boat services returned to Southampton, only to be moved back to Poole in January 1940. At Poole, a workforce of around 400 was employed including stevedores and foreman stevedores, and a novel sight for that period were the seawomen employed to help crew the launches. By November 1940 BOAC's Marine Section at Poole had on charge a number of motor launches, some of which were used for ferrying passengers to and from the flying boats, others as rescue craft, and others for general duties. When a flying boat alighted at Poole a launch transferred the passengers to the harbour, around ¾ mile away. A fuel barge then came alongside and engineers went aboard to assist with the refuelling and rectify any reported defects. Riggers then attached a 4in diameter cable to a hook under the rear of the hull and secured the other end of the cable to help steady the aircraft

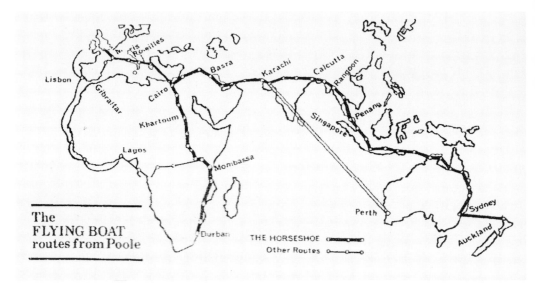

A sketch map of the flying-boat services operated out of Poole during the Second World War. (Poole Flying-Boat Celebration)

while the engines were being worked on. When the aircraft was ready to taxi out again the pilot would pull a lever to release the cable, which the riggers would pull hand over hand into their boat.

The entry of Italy into the Second World War denied safe access to the Mediterranean to Allied commercial aircraft, and in June 1940 the terminal point for BOAC's flying boat services to and from the Far East was relocated to Durban in South Africa for use on what became known as the Horseshoe route. From the Durban base at the Congella Basin the BOAC 'Empire' flying boats flew to Singapore via Mozambique, Kenya, Uganda, the Sudan, Egypt, Bahrain, India, Burma and Thailand. At Singapore the C-class flying boats of Qantas took over for the rest of the journey. Seventeen BOAC flying boats that were positioned to the south or east of Cairo at this time were ferried to the new Durban base, and three more were sent out from Poole to join them. The necessary ground staff travelled out by sea, and once the base had been established the initial weekly flight frequency was doubled. A link with Britain was maintained by using converted RAF Sunderland machines on flights down the west coast of Africa to Lagos. To avoid interception by the Luftwaffe they first flew westwards from Poole to Foynes in Ireland. Here they waited for nightfall before undertaking the long leg to Lisbon in neutral Portugal. After a day in Portugal the aircraft and their loads of diplomatic mail, civil servants and military personnel made another night-time flight, to Lagos via Bathurst and Freetown. From Lagos they flew inland, following the Congo River, and connecting at Khartoum with the service to Calcutta. Facilities aboard the flying boats were spartan, and often no steward was carried, his duties being carried out by the purser. With variations as the wartime situation changed, this routeing was to be maintained for the next seven years, with the burden on BOAC's hard-pressed aircraft being eased from October 1941 when Qantas agreed to extend its westbound services to Karachi instead of Singapore. By the spring of 1941 the BOAC C-class Empire flying boat fleet was undergoing conversion to Austerity Standard interior configuration. The removal of all luxury fittings and the installation of bench seating on the promenade deck and in the spar cabins allowed the passenger capacity to be increased to thirty.

In addition to maintaining the Horseshoe route to Singapore the BOAC machines were also called upon to undertake special duties in Europe and further afield. On the evening of 5 August 1940 *Clyde* was at her moorings at Poole when her captain, A.C. Lorraine, received instructions to ready her for departure to Lagos the following day carrying some priority passengers. These turned out to be staff officers of General de Gaulle's newly formed Free French movement. The first leg of the journey took them to Lisbon without incident. At nightfall Captain Lorraine prepared for take-off along the flarepath with a total load of 53,000lb, the heaviest weight a C-class aircraft had ever been asked to lift. During the take-off run the lights of a fishing vessel were spotted dead ahead. Avoiding action was taken and the crew managed to take off successfully, thinking that they had narrowly avoided a collision. The aircraft flew on through the night on the 1,900-mile leg to Bathurst, and at daybreak the co-pilot went below to speak to the passengers. While he was in the passenger cabin he saw through a window that a large V-shaped gash had been made on the underside of the starboard wing, and a whole section of aileron had been torn off. They had not missed the fishing boat after all! After a flight of almost fifteen hours they landed safely at Bathurst and naval engineers made temporary repairs to the wing. On the following day the flying boat continued onward to Freetown, where refuelling was accomplished using drums of petrol brought alongside in canoes. This laborious process took all day, and Lagos was finally reached the next morning. The whole journey had been carried out in strict radio

The control tower extension added to a building at the flying-boat base in Ireland. (Foynes Flying-Boat and Maritime Museum)

silence, and no weather reports had been received since Lisbon. The crew then received orders to fly the leader of the delegation on to Leopoldville in the Belgian Congo for negotiations with the Vichy French officers in Brazzaville across the Congo River. No flying boat had previously alighted on that stretch of water, but a safe landing was made, and the talks resulted in a coup that brought French Equatorial Africa over to the Allied side and ensured safe passage by air to the Middle East.

When German paratroops invaded Crete in 1941 two BOAC C-class flying boats were camouflaged to resemble more warlike RAF Short Sunderlands and made thirteen round trips between Alexandria and the Greek island, evacuating Allied troops.

In October 1940 the flying boats *Clare* and *Clyde* had been assigned to duties on the West African route. *Clyde* was at her moorings at Lisbon on the night of 14/15 February 1941 when the city was struck by a severe storm. The only occupant of the flying boat was a Portuguese watchman, who could not be evacuated by boat because of the sea state. After several hours of being battered by the elements the aircraft had its port float punctured by debris and a fierce gust lifted up the starboard wing. The aircraft capsized, with the loss of the unfortunate watchman. *Clare* maintained the services single-handedly until she was joined by a Catalina flying boat in March 1941. During the following two months two more C-class aircraft and another Catalina were assigned to the route, but there was still insufficient capacity to meet the demand. This led to the purchase of three Boeing 314A flying boats from Pan American Airways at a price of £259,250 each. In order to be able to fly non-stop from Poole to Takoradi if war conditions required they were fitted with enlarged fuel tankage, giving them a maximum cruising range of 4,500 miles. The aircraft were delivered to BOAC between May and July 1941, but facilities for the maintenance of this new type were not available in the UK, so the airline set up an engineering base for them in Baltimore. After each round trip to Africa the Boeings were ferried across the Atlantic for attention. BOAC went on to utilise these empty legs to set up a transatlantic service, flying to Baltimore via Foynes or Lisbon, Bathurst, Belem, Trinidad, and Bermuda. The winter frequency was once-weekly in each direction, increasing in the summer to four weekly trips over the shorter northerly routeing via Foynes and Botwood. In 1943 an agreement between the Canadian government and the Province of Newfoundland saw some of the wooden buildings used by the anti-aircraft battery at Botwood, and known as the Caledonia Camp, being handed over to BOAC for use as restaurant and rest facilities for transatlantic passengers during their one-and-a-half-hour refuelling stop. One prominent passenger carried across the Atlantic by the BOAC Boeings was the British Prime Minister Winston Churchill. On 16 January 1942 he flew from Virginia to Bermuda in G-AGCA *Berwick*. During the flight he took a turn at the controls and was so impressed by the aircraft that he would travel in it all the way to the UK instead of continuing his journey by warship as planned, thus saving him valuable time. After consultations with the flying boat crew a signal was sent to all en route radio stations, advising of an estimated arrival at Pembroke Dock at 0900hrs on 17 January after a journey time of seventeen and a half hours. As dawn broke the crew began their descent from 10,000ft, and fifty minutes later the aircraft was nearing Land's End at 1,000ft. However, from there on the weather deteriorated, and with visibility at Pembroke Docks reported as being down to 500yd the crew changed course and headed for RAF Mount Batten at Plymouth. After one missed approach there a safe landing was accomplished, and Churchill went on to use another BOAC Bristol 314A *Bristol* for a trip to the USA in July 1942.

The three G-class Empire flying boats ordered for Imperial Airways for transatlantic routes had not entered service by the time war broke out. They were impressed into the RAF, modified to incorporate gun turrets, radar equipment and a weapons bay, and were used on long-range North Atlantic patrol work until the end of 1941 when the two surviving examples were converted back to passenger configuration and used on services between Poole and Lagos. On 9 January 1943 G-AFCK *Golden Horn* caught fire during an air test and crashed into the River Tagus near Lisbon. In 1944 the sole survivor, G-AFCI *Golden Hind*, was completely rebuilt as a thirty-eight-seater and used on routes from Durban to Lourenço Marques, Beira and Mombasa, and from Kisumu in Kenya to the Seychelles. During September 1943 the BOAC Boeing 314As were additionally assigned to a Lisbon–Foynes–Poole–Foynes–Lisbon shuttle run, but on 29 April 1944 the type was withdrawn from the UK–West Africa route and was thereafter used exclusively on North Atlantic services.

The C-class flying boats maintained their West Africa services throughout, and on 14 September 1942 *Clare* was operating the homeward leg of a journey to Lagos when it took off from Bathurst with thirteen passengers and six crew on board. An hour or so later a radio message reporting engine problems was transmitted and twenty-five minutes later this was followed by an SOS call advising of a fire. There was no further contact with the aircraft

Pan American Boeing 314 NC18603 *Yankee Clipper* moored at Foynes in Ireland. (Foynes Flying-Boat and Maritime Museum)

and no survivors were found. With the fall of Singapore in February 1942 and the Japanese capture of Palembang in Sumatra the link to the Far East was severed, and BOAC aircraft only operated the Horseshoe route as far as Calcutta before returning to Durban.

On 19 July 1943 the BOAC C-class flying boat *Cameronian* was refuelling at Dar es Salaam whilst en route from Cairo to Durban with twenty-five passengers when the crew were asked to keep a lookout during their next leg for survivors or debris from a torpedoed British merchant ship. They spotted a lifeboat with about twenty men on board and tried dropping food and water to them in a mailbag, but the survivors were too weak to pull it into the boat. Despite being on a scheduled service with passengers aboard, the crew of the flying boat decided that they had no option but to set the aircraft down near the lifeboat and try to haul the occupants aboard using ropes. Only three of them were strong enough to successfully assist in their rescue in this way, so all the aircraft's remaining food and water, plus blankets and signal rockets, were transferred across to the lifeboat before *Cameronian* took off and headed for Mozambique. By the next morning the remaining occupants of the lifeboat, plus others found adrift in rafts, had been picked up by ships, and so the flying boat crew and their passengers resumed their scheduled route to Durban.

Once North Africa had been liberated in 1942 BOAC's No. 4 Line operated converted Sunderlands from Poole through to Cairo, from where connections were available to Calcutta, Khartoum and Lagos. On occasions as many as five or six flying boats would be moored at Cairo at the same time.

In August 1941 Pan American Airways signed a contract with the US War Department for the provision of air transport services between the USA and West Africa by a subsidiary called Pan American Airways (Africa), using both flying boats and landplanes. The contract also called for the establishment of bases along the route at San Juan, Port-au-Spain, Belem and Natal. On 7 December 1941, as the Japanese attack on Pearl Harbor was in progress, the Pan American Boeing 314 NC18609 *Pacific Clipper* was in the air between Noumea and Auckland. As the airline's Pacific route system was now out of bounds the aircraft returned to Noumea and then set off on an epic journey back to the USA via such unusual stopovers as Australia, the Trucial Oman, the Red Sea, the Nile and Congo rivers, Nigeria, and Brazil. The *Pacific Clipper* finally alighted at the La Guardia Marine Terminal in New York on 6 January 1942. Commercial services over Pan American's Pacific route network were not to be resumed until June 1946.

In 1942 Pan American's three remaining Boeing 314s were impressed into military service, initially being taken over by the United States Army Air Force, and then passed on to the US Navy. The aircraft were still operated by Pan American crews, but the allocation of seats on passenger flights became the responsibility of the US War Department. The Pan American base at Treasure Island, San Francisco, was taken over by the US Navy, with the Boeing Clippers now using it under military control. One example, NC18612 *Capetown Clipper*, was transferred across from the Pacific Division for North Atlantic duties. On 11 January 1943 Boeing 314 NC18605 *Dixie Clipper*, accompanied by NC18604 *Atlantic Clipper* as a radio communications aircraft, conveyed US President Franklin D. Roosevelt and his advisors from Miami via Trinidad and Belem to Bathurst, where they transferred to C-54 landplanes and flew to Casablanca for a conference with Winston Churchill, the Free French leader Charles de Gaulle, and the Soviet Union's Joseph Stalin.

In September 1943 the Pan American flying boats were operating between the USA and Foynes in Ireland via a stop at Botwood in Newfoundland. Three round trips were carried out each week, with reservations on the legs between Botwood and Foynes and vice versa being

BOAC Boeing 314A G-AGCB *Bangor* moored at Foynes. (Foynes Flying-Boat and Maritime Museum)

limited to sixteen passengers to ensure that each of them had a guaranteed sleeper berth. However, Pan American was not the only US airline flying the Atlantic. Despite objections from Pan American, American Export Airlines had been granted approval for services linking the United States, France and Portugal. On 20 June 1942 the airline had operated its inaugural transatlantic service between Port Washington (New York), Botwood and Foynes, using a Vought-Sikorsky VS-44 flying boat. During that month its VS-44A NC41880 *Excalibur 1*, under the command of the company's chief pilot Charles Blair, omitted the usual refuelling stop at Botwood and flew non-stop from Foynes to New York in twenty-five hours forty minutes, becoming the first commercial non-stop service from Europe to New York. From September 1943 the eastbound services continued onwards to Port Lyautey in Morocco, and the company had ambitious plans to increase its service frequency and to make Poole its European base, but in 1945 it was to be absorbed into American Airlines.

During the period August 1942–July 1943 more than 1,400 flying boat movements, carrying around 1,500 passengers, passed through Foynes, and the facilities there were being expanded to cope with the volume of traffic. Between April 1942 and 1945 American Export Airlines alone completed 405 crossings from Foynes to New York on behalf of the US Navy Air

Transport Service, and on 18 August 1945 Foynes handled a record number of passengers in a single day. The Pan American Boeing 314s NC18604 *Atlantic Clipper* and NC18605 *Dixie Clipper* both arrived from New York and returned there the same night, with a total of 101 passengers passing through the terminal on that date. However, this proved to be the swansong of the flying boat base. That autumn Pan American discontinued operations through Foynes, with the final service being operated by NC18609 *Pacific Clipper* under the command of Captain Wallace Cuthbertson. Since 1939 the Pan American fleet had made 2,097 Atlantic crossings via Foynes. BOAC was to continue transatlantic flying boat services for a few months longer. Its Boeing 314As maintained a weekly frequency to the USA until 7 March 1946, when G-AGCA *Berwick* with Captain B.C. Frost in command departed Poole for Baltimore. The airline's three Boeings were then transferred to the Baltimore–Bermuda route. *Bristol* had completed 203 Atlantic crossings, *Berwick* 201, and *Bangor* 196.

# 5

# RETURN TO PEACETIME OPERATIONS

Shortly after the end of the Second World War Pan American lost Boeing 314 NC18601 *Honolulu Clipper*. The aircraft was operating a Honolulu–San Francisco leg with twelve passengers, all naval officers, aboard on 3 November 1945. Seven hours into the flight the starboard inner engine cut out. The crew decided to turn back to Honolulu, but one and a half hours later the starboard outer engine also failed. Fuel was dumped, and some cargo and mail was jettisoned, but they were still unable to maintain altitude. They managed to alight on the sea without further damage and the aircraft remained afloat. Prior to landing the crew had sent radio messages to Pan American in Honolulu and San Francisco, and also to sister fleet member *California Clipper* that was in the vicinity. Ships soon arrived and took on board the passengers, and the escort carrier USS *Manila Bay* took the flying boat in tow, but the line parted. Further attempts at towing were also unsuccessful and the aircraft sustained damage in the process, so the salvage operation was called off. The *Honolulu Clipper* was deemed to be a potential hazard to shipping, and on 7 November 1945 she was sunk by naval gunfire.

The post-war era saw BOAC still convinced that, for the short-term at least, flying boats still provided the best option for passenger services to Africa and the Far East. They were, however, short of such machines. Of the forty-two Empire flying boats constructed only sixteen had survived the hostilities. As a stopgap measure the Short Sunderlands the airline had operated during the war with rudimentary bench-seat accommodation were re-engined with more powerful Pegasus 38 powerplants and had their interiors modified to carry twenty-two passengers, with sleeping berths for

A BOAC Short Solent taxies past the *Empire Medway* ship in harbour. (via author)

sixteen of them. The first example to be modified was G-AGJM, which was named *Hythe*. This was also used as the class name for all such conversions, eighteen of which were carried out by BOAC's own engineers at Hythe, and a further four by Short Bros at Belfast. At the end of 1945 the sole surviving G-class machine, G-AFCI *Golden Hind*, also made the journey to Belfast, for extensive overhaul and refurbishing as a luxurious twenty-four-seater. The remaining C-class flying boats continued in service on the routes to Africa, where they were also used by the BOAC training school based on the Vaal River near Johannesburg. As well as aircraft, the airline was also short of aircrew and placed advertisements in the aviation press for fifty additional flying boat pilots.

The Hythe-class Sunderland conversions had been earmarked for the reopening of schedules through to Australia and the Far East in 1946, but until then they were utilised on the routes from Poole to Karachi and Calcutta via Cairo and Bahrain. At Poole, the health, customs and immigration formalities were carried out in the borrowed premises of Carters Potteries, overlooking the quayside. During 1945 a total of 11,641 passengers arrived at Poole aboard 463 flights. Those requiring overnight accommodation were booked into the Harbour Heights Hotel and the Sandiacres Hotel. Within thirty minutes of the passengers going ashore at Poole their aircraft was flown to Hythe and brought out of the water for maintenance during the three-day turnaround time between flights. One passenger travelling home on the flying boat service in 1945 was Jeremy Cutler, a 12 year old returning from Africa with his mother and brother. They set off from Dar es Salaam on VE Day, and were scheduled to fly all the way to the UK by flying boat, along with their fellow passengers, who included the fabulously wealthy Aga Khan. They reached Khartoum via stops at Mombasa and Entebbe, but along the way their aircraft was plagued by technical problems, and at Khartoum they were transferred to a Dakota landplane for the rest of the journey.

At the beginning of 1946 two services each week were still being operated over the Horseshoe route between Durban and Calcutta, a journey that took five weeks for the round trip and necessitated night stops along the way at Lourenço Marques, Beira, Kindi, Dar es Salaam, Mombasa, Kisumu, Port Bell, Laropi, Malakal, Khartoum, Wadi Halfa, Luxor, Cairo, Kallia, Habbaniyah, Basra, Bahrain, Dubai, Karachi, Rajsamand, Gwalior, and Allahabad. However, from 13 January 1947 the Horseshoe route out of Durban only operated as far as Cairo, and on 2 March that year the Durban–Cairo leg was also withdrawn. On 31 January 1946 BOAC reopened through services

A postcard view of three BOAC Hythe-class Sunderlands (with G-AGIA *Haslemere* nearest camera) at their moorings. (via author)

BOAC Short Solent 2 G-AHIN *Southampton* berthed at one of the pontoons at Berth 50 at Southampton. (via Poole Flying-Boat Celebration)

to Singapore using Hythe-class aircraft on a thrice-weekly basis, and the C-class flying boats were retired. On 12 March 1947 G-ADHM *Caledonia*, under the command of Captain Peter Horne, flew from Durban to Poole on the final C-class service out of Africa. The remainder of the fleet were then ferried to Poole for disposal, and most of them were scrapped at Hythe. One example was offered to the Science Museum for preservation, and another to Poole Council, but, sadly, both offers were declined. After G-ADHL *Canopus* was scrapped at Hythe in November 1946, part of the aircraft's control yoke was presented to the Canopus Inn in Rochester, Kent, by Captain H. W. Alger, the Manager of BOAC's No. 4 Line, who had regularly flown the aircraft in service.

BOAC had been considering extending the Singapore flying boat services through to Australasia, and during the period 17 February–2 April 1946 had sent the Hythe-class G-AGJM on a 35,313-mile route survey trip out of Poole that took in Hong Kong, Shanghai, Tokyo, Australia and New Zealand. Among the party on board was the Chairman of BOAC, Lord Knollys. In the course of the tour the Hythe became the first British commercial

BOAC Short Solent 2 G-AHIN *Southampton* at Berth 50, Southampton Docks. (via Poole Flying-Boat Celebration)

flying boat to visit China and Japan, alighting on the Whang-Poo River in Shanghai and on the Bay of Tokyo. On 12 May 1946 BOAC, in association with Qantas, inaugurated the first post-war flying boat services between the UK and Australia. The twice-weekly service took five and a half days, with the eastbound journey routeing via Marseilles, Augusta (Sicily), Cairo, Basra, Bahrain, Karachi, Calcutta, Rangoon, Penang, Singapore (where Qantas took over responsibility for the rest of the journey), Surabaya, Darwin, and Bowen. Along the way BOAC made use of some unusual ground facilities such as a floating dock (the only one of its kind along the route) at Korangi, Karachi, and a houseboat that was used as a passenger reception lounge at Willingdon Bridge, Calcutta. Whilst flying over the city of Rangoon the passengers could obtain an aerial view of the Great Dagon Pagoda, one of the most important shrines for Buddhist pilgrims.

During 1946 a magazine article recorded the impressions of Mrs Bridgman, a passenger on a Hythe-class service to Australia:

At 0600hrs on 4th August the twelve passengers were transferred by coach from the Harbour Heights Hotel in Poole to the flying-boat terminal. Here we were handed our tickets showing our allocated seating positions and were taken by launch to the aircraft and settled down in very comfortable chairs. Following take-off we headed across France, with tea and cakes being served as we headed for Marseilles. Unfortunately the flight became very bumpy as we crossed the mountains, and several passengers succumbed to air-sickness. After the stop at Marseilles we proceeded onwards to Augusta in Sicily. During that leg of the journey a lunch of tomato soup, fish, chicken and salad, followed by ice cream and cheese and biscuits was served to those who still had the stomach for such things. A fine view of Mount Etna was obtained just before alighting at Augusta, where we went ashore for dinner but could

only stay for one hour as the aircraft had to
be airborne again before darkness fell. When we
went back on board we saw that all the bunks
had been made up, and I found that I was
sharing a compartment with two other ladies.
The next morning we were woken by the steward
at 3am, got dressed and made ready to go ashore
at Cairo. Here, our passports were examined and
we were taken to a lovely houseboat where we
could enjoy a bath followed by a breakfast of
melon, bacon and (three!) eggs, tomatoes, and
lots of chips, bread and butter and jam. All this
was quite a treat for travellers from Britain
where food rationing was still in force. The
next stop was at Basra, where a new crew took
over, and then it was on to Bahrain and then
Karachi. Here, the flying-boat alighted about
twelve miles from the city at 1.45am. We were
conveyed ashore and to an RAF camp for a meal
and a sleep in a bed on land for a change.

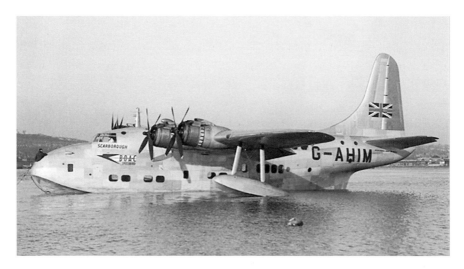

BOAC Short Solent 2 G-AHIM *Scarborough* at her moorings. (via author)

Unfortunately, the remainder of the pages from her journal have been lost and so her narrative has to end at this point.

On 30 September 1946 the refurbished G-class Empire flying boat G-AFCI *Golden Hind* returned to BOAC service on a weekly schedule from Poole to Cairo via Marseilles and Augusta. The inaugural service was commanded by Captain Dudley Travers, but the aircraft's time back in operation was to be brief. She was withdrawn from the route on 21 September 1947, as by then a new flying boat type had entered BOAC service. Back in 1945, before the Hythe class commenced operations, one of the original civilianised Sunderland 3s, G-AGKX, had been sent to Short Bros for remodelling as a commercial airliner. It retained its basic airframe, but the hull was reshaped and the original nose was replaced by a smoothly faired-over one similar to those on the Empire flying boats and a neat tailcone replaced the rear gun turret. Power was provided by four 1,030hp Bristol Pegasus 38 engines. On 28 November 1945 the remodelled aircraft emerged from the workshops as the first Short Sandringham 1. She was relaunched in a ceremony performed by the Minister of Civil Aviation Lord Winster, and during the week that followed many VIPs, including Mr Hudson Fysh, the managing director of Qantas, were carried aloft on short demonstration flights. Now bearing the name *Himalaya*, the aircraft participated in the Victory Air Pageant at Eastleigh Airport, Southampton, on 22 June 1946.

The Sandringham 1 had accommodation for twenty-two seated passengers or sixteen in sleeper berths on its lower deck, which also contained dressing rooms and a promenade cabin. On the upper deck was the cocktail bar, buffet, and a galley with refrigerator and steam oven, and an eight-seat dining room whose settee-style seating could be converted into upper and lower bunks for four additional sleeper passengers. Short Bros was hopeful

An aerial view of the Marine Air Terminal at Southampton. A Short Solent is on one of the pontoons, and a Hythe-class Sunderland is in mid-stream. The ocean liner *Queen Elizabeth* is berthed at the Ocean Terminal beyond. (Solent Sky Museum)

A BOAC Short Solent overflies the Marine Air Terminal and Berth 50 at Southampton. (via author)

of persuading BOAC to adopt the Sandringham as its standard equipment on the Empire route network, but no immediate order was forthcoming as the airline had plans to switch to new landplane types in the near future. To tide the airline over until then the Hythe-class soldiered on. On 24 August 1946 they inaugurated weekly 'Dragon' services to Hong Kong, and on connecting flights to Bangkok, Singapore, Okinawa, and Iwakuni in Japan. By 1947 delivery delays with the airline's hoped-for new landplane types forced BOAC to rethink its plans, and it requested the Ministry of Civil Aviation to order nine examples of the Sandringham 5 on its behalf as an interim measure. This was a conversion of the Short Sunderland 5, powered by 1,200hp Pratt & Whitney Twin Wasp engines conferring a cruising speed of 176mph and a range of 2,450 miles. Known in BOAC use as the Plymouth class, they entered service on 2 May 1947, replacing the Hythe class on weekly services from Poole to Bahrain and Kuwait and later operating through to Hong Kong.

On the night of 22/23 August 1947 BOAC suffered its first flying boat passenger fatalities since November 1943. The Sandringham 5 G-AHZB

*Portland* was operating a Hong Kong–Poole schedule and was attempting a night landing at Bahrain Marine Air Base when it crashed with the loss of ten of its twenty-six occupants. One of the hazards faced by the flying boat crews during take-off was the fore-and-aft rocking effect known as 'porpoising'. This occurred when the forces operating on the underside of the hull shifted from the rear to the front. The aircraft might then leave the water for a few seconds before touching down again heavily, often with such force that an engine might cut out. The pilots' operating manual advised that at the first hint of porpoising a backward force should be applied to the control wheel and held there firmly. The workload of the UK-based pilots was a gruelling one. On the route to the Far East they could be away for up to thirty-eight days at a time, although this was compensated for by periods of home leave of thirty days or more.

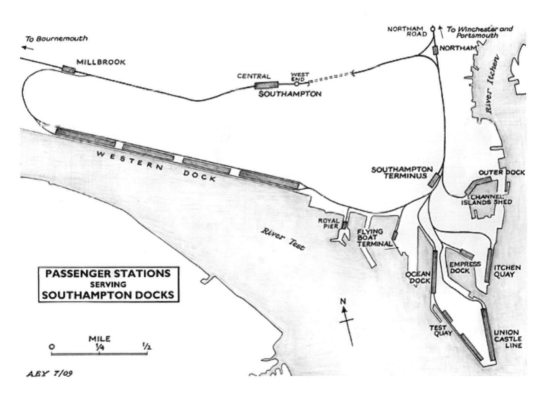

A map of part of the docks at Southampton, showing the locations of the Marine Air Terminal and the railway stations serving the docks. (via Poole Flying-Boat Celebration)

One of the stopping points along the route to the Orient was Basra, situated at the confluence of the Tigris and Euphrates rivers. Here was sited an elegant passenger building with a landplane airfield on one side and on the other the Shatt al-Arab, where the flying boats alighted. Along the routes to Australia and the Far East BOAC had a fleet of around 200 marine support craft distributed between nearly thirty bases and manned by 700 trained staff. These were under the command of the Marine Superintendent Mr B. Smith and his deputy, both of whom had worked with marine craft since Imperial Airways introduced the Empire flying boats in 1936. Assisting them were some thirty coxwains, boatswains, and marine officers. Two of these possessed master's certificates, and several more held first or second mate's certificates. All of them had served tours of duty in distant and isolated overseas locations. It became the custom that as the launch carrying the passengers from the flying boats arrived or departed the shore the uniformed BOAC marine craft men would turn out on the quayside in parade ground order.

By 1947 the cost of maintaining BOAC's flying boat facilities at home and throughout the Empire had risen to more than £1 million per annum. The base at Poole was becoming too costly to operate, and the alighting areas there were too constricted and congested with pleasure craft. Also, the Southern Railway had announced that it was no longer financially viable for it to provide BOAC with a dedicated carriage on the appropriate London–Poole services and it was discontinuing the practice. To replace this facility BOAC switched to road transport and acquired four specially modified Leyland coaches for use on transfers that included a stop at Basingstoke in each direction.

The Pakenham Committee had been set up to examine possible sites for a new permanent flying boat terminal in the UK, and by October 1947 it had come up with a shortlist of three potential locations. These were: Cliffe, Chichester Harbour, or the estuary of the Blackwater River. As it was likely to take some time to reach a decision and then construct the facilities at the chosen site it was decided that BOAC would as a temporary measure transfer its flying boat services back to Southampton. The final BOAC services in and out of Poole took place on 30 March 1948, and on the following day the airline's flying boat base was officially transferred to Southampton. The first post-war service from there was operated to Australia by the Hythe-class aircraft G-AGEW *Hanwell* on 1 April. The BOAC terminal and offices at Salterns, Poole, were vacated by the airline and eventually taken over by the Poole Harbour Yacht Club. A site at Berth 50 in Southampton's Eastern Docks had been selected for the interim terminal, which was intended to be a temporary structure with a projected life of five years, until a new National Marine Airport had become operational at whichever location had been selected. However, the facilities at Berth 50 were not ready when BOAC transferred operations, and so for the time being the airline used Berth 108, close to the ocean liner terminal. A new contender for the interim flying boat base had also emerged. Arguments for the use of Portsmouth instead of Southampton had centred on the premise that the Royal Beach Hotel at nearby Southsea could be leased by BOAC for its flying boat headquarters, thus saving the cost (estimated at £80,000) of erecting temporary buildings at Southampton. Other advantages put forward included the existence of fast electric train services between Portsmouth and London, plus an existing arterial road adjacent to the proposed flying boat terminal, and the presence of Portsmouth's landplane airport, which could be used for feeder flights to and from other parts of the UK. In the event, none of the proposals for alternative sites came to fruition, and BOAC was to remain at Southampton until the end of its flying boat operations.

On 14 April 1948 the interim terminal at Berth 50 at Southampton was officially opened by the Minister of Civil Aviation, Lord Nathan, cutting a white ribbon stretched from the terminal building to one of the floating pontoons that had eliminated the need for launch transfers to and from the aircraft. In his speech, Lord Nathan referred to the difficulties encountered in finding suitable sites for marine aircraft bases along the Empire routes, as such locations needed to possess clear landing approaches and plenty of manoeuvring space, and had to be close to centres of population. He also wondered whether the passengers of the future would prefer to travel on the roomy but slow flying boats or on a new generation of speedy but less comfortable landplanes. The occasion was also used for the christening of BOAC's new Short Solent flying boat as *Southampton* by the Mayoress of Southampton using a silver jug filled with Empire wine, and for the presentation of a ship's chronometer to the aircraft. The new building had sufficient capacity to handle flying boat arrivals and departures simultaneously. On the ground floor was a reception lounge and customs facilities, and covered walkways to the pontoons and the railway station. Upstairs, a sixty-eight-seat restaurant and lounge bar ran the full length of the terminal's façade and offered pleasant views over Southampton Water. Also on the first floor were the offices of the BOAC Station Superintendent and the local Ministry of Civil Aviation representative. The control tower was sited at one end of the terminal building, and the airline's maintenance base was now only about half a mile away across the water at Hythe, so the costly ferry flights from Poole were eliminated. When an aircraft alighted at Southampton it was taxied up to a buoy, to which its radio officer secured the bow mooring rope. A launch was then positioned so that its crew could attach the aircraft's stern release hook to two cables, which were then used to winch the flying boat tail-first into the fork of one of the floating pontoons. If it became likely that a departure from Southampton was going to be significantly delayed, a message was sent through to Airways House in London, and refreshments and sometimes entertainment of some kind would be provided for the passengers waiting there. On occasions a tea dance would even be laid on for them in the building's art deco ballroom.

In the meantime, the introduction of long-distance landplanes such as the Lockheed Constellation across the Atlantic had rendered the marine base at Foynes in Ireland almost redundant. The last BOAC flying boat to call there was the Hythe-class G-AGJC *Humber* on 24 March 1946, and on 5 April that year the airline announced that it was discontinuing the use of Foynes, but there was still the possibility of its flying boats staging through there again if the gigantic Saunders-Roe Princess aircraft then under development entered BOAC service.

On the Baltimore–Bermuda route the BOAC Boeing 314As were supplemented by three examples of the improved Short Sandringham 7. These were fitted with thirty seats and known as the Bermuda class. However, this was to be a short-lived arrangement, as on 17 January 1948 G-AGBZ *Bristol* operated the last BOAC Boeing 314A service, from Bermuda to Baltimore. The aircraft were sold to the US carrier World Airways Inc., which had already acquired Pan American's four remaining Boeing 314s. In BOAC service the three Boeing 314As had completed 596 transatlantic crossings and carried in the region of 42,000 passengers. The Bermuda-class Sandringhams were also withdrawn from the route, and the Darrell's Island base at Bermuda was closed down, the services from the US mainland having been taken over by Lockheed Constellation landplanes.

In March 1948 the World Airways fleet of Boeing 314s and 314As began operating irregular services on a New York–Baltimore–Puerto Rico routeing, carrying upwards of eighty passengers on each flight. In May 1948 one of these aircraft was en route from Puerto Rico to the USA with eighty-two passengers aboard when it encountered severe weather that ruled out

Poster advertising the joint Qantas/BOAC Kangaroo service to London by flying-boat or
landplane. (Qantas Heritage Collection)

a landing at either Baltimore or New York. A precautionary landing was safely accomplished at the head of the Chesapeake Bay, and the captain then elected to try to taxi the flying boat the 60 or so remaining miles to Baltimore. The aircraft ran aground on a sandbank and had to be pulled off by a tug. Undeterred, once the weather improved the captain took off and flew his passengers to their scheduled destinations. In February 1949 World Airways put its fleet of flying boats and their support equipment up for sale.

After the termination of BOAC services through Foynes, the flying boat base there had one final movement to handle. On 30 September 1947 the former Pan American Airways Boeing 314A NC18612, now operated by American International Airlines and renamed *Bermuda Sky Queen*, arrived from Poole with fifty-two passengers and a crew of seven. After a prolonged stay it departed for New York via Gander at 0145hrs on 13 October. During its Atlantic crossing the flying boat had to battle against strong headwinds, and it was still 600 miles from Gander when its crew transmitted an SOS reporting that they had insufficient fuel to reach land and were turning back in order to alight on the sea near to the US Coast Guard weather ship *Bibb*. A successful landing was made about 3 miles from the ship, and the Boeing was then taxied alongside it. All the passengers and crew were safely transferred to the *Bibb*, but the *Bermuda Sky Queen* had suffered serious damage and was eventually sunk by naval gunfire, having become a hazard to shipping.

Meanwhile, back in the UK a replacement for BOAC's elderly fleet of Hythe-class Sunderlands was under production. During the twelve months up to the end of March 1947 eleven of these aircraft had each clocked up more than 20,000 miles. Early in 1946 BOAC had been offered the opportunity to evaluate on loan the second production Short S.45 Seaford 1. This type was larger than the Sunderlands and had originally been intended for use in the war in the Pacific. With the abrupt ending of that war it was considered to have potential for civil use, and BOAC had placed an order for twelve modified examples for operation as the Short Solent 2. These aircraft were to be powered by four 1,680hp Bristol Hercules 637 engines. Up to thirty-four passengers were to be carried on two decks at a cruising speed of 244mph over a range of 1,800 miles. The first Solent for BOAC, G-AHIL *Salisbury*, was launched onto the River Medway at Rochester in Kent on 11 November 1946, and made its maiden flight on 1 December that year. Another of the BOAC Solents, G-AHIY *Southsea*, was later to become the very last aircraft to be constructed at the historic Short Bros works at Rochester.

The February 1947 *BOAC News Letter* announced that the airline was to introduce Solents onto its 'Springbok' service to South Africa in place of the current Avro York landplanes. In the announcement the BOAC Chairman Sir Harold Hartley professed himself convinced that the flying boat journey to South Africa would be the most fascinating in the world for travellers, and would offer great possibilities for tourism with its blend of historical and scenic features. The Solent was the most powerful British flying boat type to enter BOAC service. On its lower deck were situated three passenger cabins, a promenade cabin, a library, wardrobes, dressing rooms and toilets. A spiral staircase provided access from the promenade cabin to the upstairs cocktail bar, stewards' compartment and galley. The operating crew consisted of the captain, first officer, wireless operator, and flight engineer, and the passengers were looked after by the chief steward, galley steward, and stewardess. In April 1948 the Solent G-AHIN *Southampton* carried a party of journalists on a 'pre-inaugural' trip along the route to South Africa. The journey did not get off to the most auspicious of starts. After casting off from its berth at Southampton and taxiing past the moored Solents, Hythes and Sandringhams at the BOAC maintenance base at Hythe, the crew ran up the engines prior to take-off, whereupon one engine suffered a magneto drop and the aircraft had to return to its berth for attention. The journalists were obliged to disembark while the fault was rectified, and it was some seven hours later when they were able to reboard and take off. The route took them over the Normandy coastline, Avignon and Marseilles before the aircraft made a night landing at Augusta in Sicily. The night was spent in the barrack like accommodation rented by BOAC, and the next morning they flew over the ancient city of Syracuse prior to alighting at Cairo. Here, they attended a reception hosted by the local travel trade and press aboard the houseboat *Puritan*. Later that day they reboarded the flying boat for the next leg to Luxor, but before take-off was possible they were witnesses to an interesting hold-up. Two Arab feluccas were tacking down the waterway and refused to pull in to the bank and give right of way to the taxiing aircraft. The crew of the attendant fire launch then intervened and threatened to turn their hoses onto the boats. This threat had the desired effect and the flight was able to continue.

The first stewardess employed to work on the BOAC flying boats post-war was Olive Carlisle. During the Second World War she had served a short stint in August 1943 on the shuttle flights between Poole and Foynes, and in the spring of 1948 she was posted to the Solent fleet at Southampton.

She was on duty aboard G-AHIT *Severn* on the inaugural service to South Africa on 4 May that year. The BOAC flying boat flights were part of the joint BOAC/South African Airways 'Springbok' service, initially consisting of two Solent flights and one Avro York landplane service each week. For the southbound schedules she was required to report to BOAC's Airways Terminal in Buckingham Palace Road, London, at 0630hrs to greet her passengers as they arrived to check in. By 0700hrs the formalities had been completed and she escorted them on the coach journey to Southampton via a stop at the Hog's Back in Surrey for breakfast. Upon reaching Southampton the passengers were taken through to customs and emigration by BOAC traffic officers, while the cabin crew boarded the aircraft and had the cabin ready in time to show the passengers to their allotted seats. On departure it was normal practice for two engines to be started, and once these were running satisfactorily the wireless officer would cast off by operating a lever that released the wire restraining the aircraft. The remaining two engines would be started once the flying boat was taxiing. The first scheduled stop was at Augusta, where first-time flying boat passengers would sometimes be startled as the spray generated on touchdown completely obscured the windows on the lower deck. The night stop at Augusta was spent at the BOAC 'air posting house' called Canopus House, which boasted 126 rooms and a fine view over the bay. The following day was spent flying onward to Cairo and then Luxor. During their overnight stay at Luxor the passengers had the opportunity to take part in an excursion to visit the Valley of the Kings. The next day they flew to Khartoum and Port Bell, where the night stop was at Silver Springs, 5 five miles along the road to Kampala. The highlight of the following day's travel was flying over the Victoria Falls after traversing the whole length of Lake Victoria. The roar of the falls could be heard over the noise from the engines while still several miles off. The Solents alighted on a wide stretch of the Zambesi River some 4½ miles upstream. The flying boat would receive some attention here while the passengers and crew went ashore to the Victoria Falls Hotel for their final overnight stay. The construction of the landing stage, terminal facilities, and a 6-mile road linking the falls to the hotel had all been financed by the government of Southern Rhodesia, thus relieving BOAC of the considerable expense of building and maintaining a base there. The Solents could only arrive and depart during daylight hours, as night operations would necessitate the use of a flarepath, which would have invited unwelcome attention from crocodiles and hippos. The night stop at Victoria Falls soon became the high spot of the journey to South Africa, as passengers had the opportunity to visit the falls by moonlight before turning in. After a short night's sleep they were roused at 0630hrs, breakfasted with the crew, and were then taken by bus to the jetty and out to the aircraft by launch. As the Solents cruised at around 200mph at a civilised altitude of 7,000ft or so the passengers would congregate on the promenade deck to watch the wildlife and scenery passing by below. On some occasions too many people would gather there at the same time and the captain would send back a message requesting that some of them return to their seats as they were upsetting the balance of the aircraft. Flying over Africa was not always pleasant, however. Thermals could create turbulence that the unpressurised flying boats could not climb above, and airsickness was not uncommon.

The catering for the final leg of the journey was prepared and placed aboard by the Victoria Falls Hotel, and made an impressive contrast to that available back in Britain, where food rationing was still in force. Canapés and aperitifs were served, often on the promenade deck, before the silver service luncheon. Typical of the menus was the selection offered aboard G-AHIN *Southampton* en route from Victoria Falls to Vaaldam on 1 May 1948. This consisted of cold roast chicken, boiled ham, cold tongue, roast lamb and salad, followed by fruit tart and cream, cheese and biscuits, fruit and coffee. The Solents were equipped with the latest Crittall 'Airborne' electric oven, which only the chief steward was permitted to operate. The seats on the aircraft were covered in blue fabric, the carpets were of a deeper blue, and the curtains were in two shades of beige. One of the stewards' extra duties was the fastening of the bulkhead doors separating the lower deck cabins so that any water that found its way in could be contained and removed. Vaaldam was reached in the afternoon and the passengers were taken by coach on the 58-mile journey into Johannesburg. If thunderstorms rendered Vaaldam temporarily unusable there was an alternative alighting area at Haartebeeste Port, almost 30 miles equidistant from Johannesburg and Pretoria. The fare from London to Southampton to Johannesburg was set at £167 one-way or £300 12s 0d for a round trip, thus putting the trip beyond the means of all but government officials and their families, those travelling on business, and wealthy individuals.

During June 1948 the Solent fleet had to be withdrawn for float modifications, not returning to service until October. When they transited Egypt after this, they utilised the Lake Mariut Marine Base at Alexandria instead of Cairo. This artificial lake had been constructed by the Egyptian government at a cost of £125,000, and here BOAC set up stores, a marine yard, offices, engineering workshops, a staff canteen, and a kitchen in which the catering for the flying boats was prepared. There was also a restaurant and restroom offering pleasant views across the lake for the passengers. It was here that they completed the immigration and quarantine checks before passing on to the nearby control tower for customs clearance.

On 19 March 1948 the Plymouth-class Sandringham service to Hong Kong was extended to Iwakuni in Japan. The first extended service was operated by G-AJMZ *Perth*, with the 10,625-mile journey from the UK scheduled to be accomplished in seven days. From 20 November 1948 the service was extended again, this time all the way through to Tokyo, and on 30 December that year the Sandringhams began operations between Hong Kong and Shanghai, a link that later had to be suspended because of political difficulties. By the end of 1948 the timetable of BOAC flights to and from Southampton read as follows:

MON ...  1145hrs Hythe-class arrival from Australia.
1500hrs Plymouth-class arrival from Hong Kong.
TUE ...  1145hrs Solent departure to Vaaldam.
1230hrs Plymouth-class departure to Hong Kong.
WED ...  1145hrs Hythe-class departure to Australia.
1300hrs Hythe-class arrival from Karachi.
THUR ...  1145hrs Hythe-class departure to Karachi.
1500hrs Plymouth-class arrival from Tokyo.
FRI ...  1145hrs Solent departure to Vaaldam.
1230hrs Plymouth-class departure to Tokyo.
1530hrs Hythe-class departure to Australia.
SAT...  1145hrs Hythe-class departure to Australia.
1530hrs Solent arrival from Vaaldam.
SUN ...  1145hrs Solent departure to Vaaldam.
1530hrs Hythe-class arrival from Australia.
1530hrs Solent arrival from Vaaldam.

The last full year of BOAC Hythe-class operations would be 1948. On 16 February 1949 the final Hythe-operated service from Australia arrived at Southampton, with Captain D.W. Pallet in command of G-AGJO *Honduras* for the last leg. Between them, the Hythe class and the other civilianised Sunderlands had flown 25,117,246 miles and carried 79,793 passengers in BOAC service. The Plymouth–class Sandringhams were to remain in service for a little longer, but by the summer of 1949 Canadair Argonaut landplane airliners were in service. From late August they supplanted the Sandringhams on the Far East routes, while the Africa flights remained flying boat operated, using Short Solent 2s. These examples were actually owned by the Ministry of Civil Aviation and leased to BOAC, but in 1948 the decision had been taken to give BOAC its own Solents by the expedient of

BOAC Short Solent 3 G-AKNO moored on the River Thames near Tower Bridge in May 1949. (Dave Welch)

acquiring the six Short Seaford 1 flying boats under construction at Belfast and converting them to thirty-nine-seat Solent 3s for the state-owned airline. On 5 May 1949 the first Solent 3, registered G-AKNO, alighted on the River Thames near Tower Bridge and was moored on public view close to Tower Pier as part of the events commemorating the thirtieth anniversary of civil aviation in Britain. On 10 May it was moved to a new site by the Traitors' Gate at the Tower of London and was named *City of London* by the Lord Mayor of London Sir George Aylwen, who poured South African champagne over the aircraft's bows from a silver chalice. In a speech thanking the Lord Mayor, the Parliamentary Secretary to the Minister for Civil Aviation referred to the future of flying boats and the fact that BOAC was the only airline operating them. He said that although the high maintenance costs of the flying boat bases had placed the airline at an economic disadvantage, Britain had retained faith in the aircraft on the basis of their superior standards of comfort and security. Whether in the end Britain would be able to retain the flying boat services, or whether the inexorable forces of airline economics would force the country to abandon them, remained to be seen. He expressed the hope that, through BOAC's perseverance with them, other operators would be encouraged to turn to flying boats.

In April 1949 the flying boat component of the BOAC fleet consisted of eleven Solents and eleven Plymouth-class Sandringhams, the latter type on services to Karachi, Tokyo and Shanghai, and between Singapore and Hong Kong. The Solents were to serve on many routes. On 15 May 1949 the type replaced Avro York landplanes on twice-weekly services to Lake Naivasha (the alighting point for Nairobi), and on 26 May they took over from Sandringhams on the weekly services to Karachi.

During September and October 1949 one of the schedules on the South Africa service was temporarily rerouted via Cape Maclear in Nyasaland instead of Victoria Falls. BOAC had been persuaded to include Cape Maclear in its route network by the new governor of Nyasaland in order to service the Colonial Development Corporation's Tung Oil project at that location. A base at Cape Maclear had to be set up from scratch, and initially there was no jetty and no launches for the passengers, who were transported by a small dinghy to a landing place at Monkey Bay, 8 miles away. From 10 November 1949 the stops at Cape Maclear were increased to once-weekly, with the Solents passing through on Tuesdays on their way to Vaaldam and on Thursdays on the way back. By then the facilities had been improved and launches had been acquired to ferry passengers to and from the Cape Maclear Hotel. This luxury establishment boasted a golf course, billiards room, and a swimming pool, but could only be accessed by road during the dry season. The air service into Cape Maclear was short-lived, however, lasting just one year, and its withdrawal led to the closure of the hotel twelve months later. A temporary grounding of BOAC's Canadair Argonaut fleet during September and October 1949 saw Solents once again being used on the services to Basra and Bahrain, but once the Argonauts returned to service the flying boats were only used on the routes to South Africa and East Africa. At that time many of the African services carried the children of colonial officers, travelling unaccompanied out from the UK to join their parents for the school holidays. One former schoolchild later recalled travelling as a teenager to Dar es Salaam for this purpose. Over Ethiopia the crew had to climb as high as possible to try to avoid thunderstorms, but many passengers were airsick nevertheless.

By the beginning of the 1950s the days of the BOAC flying boats were numbered. On 24 September 1950 the Solent schedules into Lake Naivasha were withdrawn and replaced by Handley Page Hermes landplane services into Nairobi airport, and on 3 November that year the final Solent service to Vaaldam was operated out of Southampton by G-AHIO *Somerset*. The aircraft's arrival back at Southampton brought to an end BOAC's last flying boat service. Flying boats had been in unbroken service with BOAC and its predecessor Imperial Airways since 1924. The Solent fleet was then officially disbanded, although by then several of the aircraft had already been sold off to Aquila Airways for use on tourist services. The remainder went into storage and were eventually broken up at Hamworthy and Belfast. The sole survivor of the G class, G-AFCI *Golden Hind*, lingered on unused and unwanted until 1954, when it was damaged in a storm and subsequently scrapped.

## By Flying-Boat to Africa: A Passenger's View

At the end of November 1948 newly married Hilary Kirk emigrated to Salisbury, Southern Rhodesia, aboard the BOAC Short Solent G-AHIY *Southsea*. She had never flown or travelled abroad before. These are the letters she sent home to her parents during the course of her journey. Much emphasis is placed on the meals served during the trip, as Britain was still subject to stringent food rationing at the time.

## 28 November 1948. Grand Hotel, Lyndhurst, New Forest

We have just arrived here. We arrived at Waterloo with lots of time to spare, and travelled First Class, courtesy of BOAC. Ditto the dinner on the train, the best I've yet had on the railways … tomato soup, roast duck, cheese and celery, coffee with masses of sugar. We came here by BOAC bus, and the nice little hostess is a dear and most friendly and efficient. This looks a lovely place, but we shall be called at 6.15am tomorrow … oh dear. It's great fun, they give us a card each day with times and dates and instructions on it, all v.clear. I don't think there is a full quota of passengers. Hence the leniency over excess baggage charges, I believe.

## 30 November 1948. In flight over France, 1.05 p.m.

What a way to spend a Sunday afternoon in November! Blazing sun and clear blue sky. Cotton wool clouds and France underneath us like a jigsaw puzzle of roads, walls and hedges. No feeling of movement whatsoever. We've been up for over an hour and have just crossed the Loire, so we must be moving fast really. We got up at 6.15am only to find we needn't have bothered, as the fog caused a delay, and breakfast was at a civilised hour. We left Lyndhurst at 10am and went by bus to Southampton, where we were whisked at top speed through what formalities there were. Handed in ration books, ID cards and passports for inspection (I'll send sweets and clothing, as they gave them back to me), and merely told the customs we hadn't anything dutiable. Finally we walked along yards of jetty to the flying-boat and took our seats. Very comfy … seats adjustable for reclining or sitting up, well-padded with rug, very warm and beautifully clean and new-looking. We're in the middle cabin, under the wing, and I have a glorious view from the window. Staff v. helpful and kind. Our nice hostess is still with us. Forgot to say that as we were held up we are spending the night at Marseilles instead of Augusta. We will be there by 3.0pm. We skimmed out into the harbour, past the liners Queen Elizabeth and Durban Castle, and each engine was tried out, then we got up speed and water shot past the windows, and suddenly we lifted and shot up, gaining height v. quickly, and entered thick fog which was rather frightening as we were quite blind. But it grew lighter, and zip, we were in blazing sun with clear deep blue sky. The clouds were like icing sugar or snow, all creased and bumpy and extending to eternity, with little gaps giving a glimpse of the Channel below. We had no 'last view of England', only clouds for miles. Then, suddenly, there was the Cherbourg Peninsular and the cliffs of France, for all the world like an Ordnance Survey map, or a model for Town and Country Planning. I just can't see enough of it! Forests are ink blots and houses look so fragile. The fields are olive, not a clear green, and we can see frost on the north face of hills still. They brought us boxes of sweets to chew as we took off, to clear our ears. We had lunch at 12.30, very good stew and lovely peas and potatoes, apple tart, bread and real butter, and gorgonzola cheese. The First Officer (enormous type, with moustaches halfway up his cheeks … most odd) has just been round to see if we're OK, and he says that we're 7,500ft up and going at 194mph. He also said that our night stops have been changed, and will now be at Marseilles, Alexandria and Khartoum. I've tried to give you an idea of all this, it's so exciting, and feels so safe, no wobble at all. I've just spotted the Massif Central, and Cevennes comes next. N.B … We're provided with special maps, these airletter forms, postcards and leaflets, all free, so we can follow our course. This IS fun!

## 28 November 1948. Postcard headed Hotel L'Arbois, Marseilles

This is our first night stop. It's a wonderful place, built in 1946, so very modern. Every room has bathroom etc attached, and ours is most palatial and comfy … better than the Ritz! We've just had dinner … soup, then ham and salad, then lamb, then masses of fruit for dessert. Now we're going to visit the harbour and eat bouillabaisse, if we've room! After all, our next stop is Augusta. We had a perfect launch, and it was glorious coming over the Cevennes and then seeing the Med and Marseilles.

## 29 November 1948. In flight. 12.15 p.m. Local time. Just past Sardinia

Oh Gosh! I forgot to take a Kwell before we started, and as it's been rather bumpy just now I've regretted the omission! However, I've had one now, and a cup of coffee and some scones have made me feel far better. We left Marignane (airport for Marseilles) at 10am and were airborne by 10.15. We arrive at Augusta at 1.15 for lunch, so we'll have a lovely long afternoon and evening. Marseilles is terribly dilapidated and very French. Just like the films. Our hotel seemed to be the only clean and modern place we saw. We continue to be excellently looked after. It is very cloudy below us today, but we saw Sardinia OK. Malta we missed, I'm afraid. I don't know why it's so bumpy because the weather looks perfect. I have never seen such heavenly clouds as today. We flew among great whorls of snow white, and there were clear alleys between. They rose in mountains round us. The sun tips them with gold, silver and rose, and through a gap we can see the dull sea far below, dreary and utterly divorced from the world where we fly like gods.

## 29 and 30 November 1948. Augusta, Sicily

Monday evening … I feel impelled to tell you about each new place we reach, so you'll be inundated with letters if I keep up this rate of two a day … We had rather a nasty journey towards the end today, very bumpy and sick-making in horrid grey cloud. Then we landed and I really thought we would brush the bushes on the shore, we were so low, but we reached the sea safely to find it choppy and dark green. The weather is dismal, wet and windy. So much for sunny Italy.

Tuesday AM, in flight … No time to finish this yesterday. We landed by a jetty and walked up an Italian garden with hanging trees and cacti … hideous but fun … to BOAC House, where we had a lovely lunch. Our bedroom was in Raleigh House, up the road. A dreadfully bleak, forbidding room. We were glad to leave it this AM. In the afternoon we looked around Augusta. Very dirty, sordid and dilapidated, with rubble still in the streets, and signs of American occupation. Most unattractive, but full of beautiful children. We rose at 5.15am, of all the Godless hours, today, because we have to make up lost time and reach Luxor. The Med is very dull to fly over, and we've been at 1500ft most of the time. Africa appeared as a line on the horizon, and is now revealed as a flat desert rimmed with turquoise, and the sea is deep blue and silver in the sun. We've left all the clouds at Sicily and the sky rivals the sea, without a cloud. We've skipped forward an hour, and reach Alexandria in 15 mins. It's 12.30 and we left at 6.30, so we've taken five hours.

## 30 November 1948. Hotel Cecil, Alexandria

Tuesday evening … Well! Since I finished the last page we've had quite an eventful time. We flew over the desert and circled Alex (Alexandria), and then landed neatly on the artificial lake. We had a very good lunch at BOAC HQ, and were allowed an hour for it. Then we returned to the plane, took off, and had just reached a good height when one of the engines conked out and another began to leak oil furiously! So we had to return and land again, having been airborne for about five minutes … We were told that we would be night-stopping in Alex after all, which pleased us as we very much wanted to see something of it. The air hostess's fiancée is here, so she was thrilled to bits, bless her. We had a beastly time with the Egyptian customs. They searched all our night cases and were very suspicious. Then we had a lovely bus ride into Alex itself, along the promenade. To our joy, we found this hotel (an enormous place) overlooks the beautiful bay, and we have a room on the 5th floor with a balcony overlooking it too. It has a lovely bathroom attached, and as the cost is £2 per day in piastres you can see that BOAC doesn't stint us. No wonder they make losses … The set-up is that if the plane isn't ready we transfer to another, crew and all, and leave at 2pm for Khartoum. If the plane is OK we leave earlier than that, but not at another Godless hour, so we're having breakfast in bed!

## 1 and 2 December. Wednesday 4 p.m., now on board Short Solent 2 G-AHIM Scarborough

We are now flying over the desert, a dreary but rather impressive prospect. The sun is tremendously hot. The men are all in open shirts and the crew have put on tropical uniform. We have crossed the Nile, which looked very dirty, and saw the pyramids outside Cairo, just like haystacks! The desert and the fertile belt are so clearly delineated that it seems as if a line has been ruled between them. Last night we had a look around Alex, but couldn't see much in the dark, and everything was dreadfully expensive. It was a glorious, starry night, and the harbour is, I think, one of the most beautiful things I have seen, either by day or night. So symmetrical, with no piers to spoil its lines, and the stately tall buildings looking out over it. We had breakfast in bed at 8.30 as a change from early rising, and were thrilled to have about a month's ration of bacon and two fried eggs each, as well as heaps of butter and lovely white rolls. So far I haven't tired of white bread! And the idea of having sugar and butter ad lib hasn't penetrated properly yet. There was an anti-British demonstration going on in town, and we were warned not to go out. I would have liked to have seen some agitators etc, but we couldn't see a thing from our window. Most disappointing … I forgot to tell you that we flew past Etna, veiled in mist, outside Augusta. Most of these geographical curiosities are rather disappointing, I think. I get far more of a kick out of seeing palm trees, banana bushes, natives in queer costumes, and sleeping under mosquito nets, watching the silly little houses and fields as we fly low, and drinking coffee in cafes and watching the life outside. We left Alex after lunch at 1pm in buses, and no stones were thrown! Customs again were a nuisance. We are in the other plane now… It's exactly the same. We're dropping down to Luxor now, so I'll stop.

Thursday. We landed at sunset and Luxor looked very exotic, with palms, temple ruins and houses outlined against the beautiful sky. We walked to our night stop, the Luxor Hotel. We had a very bare but quite comfy room with two washbasins, and shared a bathroom with the Captain in the room beyond. We saw from our flight cards to our horror that we had to rise again at 5am. We went to bed at 9.30pm and crawled out again at five. We took off at 6.30am and touched down in Khartoum at 10.15 to refuel. We were outside of the town and saw nothing as we only stayed for about half an hour.

# 2 and 3 December

Thursday 4.15 p.m. It was glorious weather outside Khartoum, hot and cloudless with a strong warm wind blowing. We thought of you in England as far as weather goes, and wouldn't swap for anything! We have excellent breakfasts on board. Today we had eggs, tomato and bacon. Another day we had ham and eggs. The lunches and teas are also marvellous. We followed the Nile for hundreds of miles. This has been our longest day's flying. We thought we would never leave the desert, but now we have been over equatorial jungle for some time. I went fast asleep all afternoon. It's cool in the plane as we're flying high. We are nearly at Kampala now. The part I like least about flying is coming in to land. I always feel the plane will touch the ground before the water. And although our Captain brings us down very gently my tummy is inclined to remain aloft! Actually, he always makes beautiful landings, so I needn't worry. My ears give me very little trouble, merely getting a little stuffy as we change height, but nothing that blowing won't cure. We can see Lake Victoria now and we're dropping fast, so I'll stop.

Friday 9.30 a.m. Kampala was the most exotic of all our night stops. Almost on the equator, it was very warm and humid. We were divided into two parties, with some of us going to the Imperial Hotel, a large modern one, I gather. We were taken to Silver Springs. This was a little 'village' of bungalows with a main building for eating in. Rather 'a la Butlins', we were allotted two little rooms in one bungalow. Very clean and nicely furnished. We dressed in one and slept in the other. Both had stone wash basins. In due course we departed Kampala, and about ten minutes after getting airborne the Captain made the plane give a large lurch to signify that we had 'crossed the line' (the equator). Later we were each given a huge certificate, quite barmy, stating that as we'd 'shot the biggest line in the world we were now qualified as members of the Winged Order of Line-Shooters, signed Phoebus Apollo, Empyrean Emperor'. Lake Victoria is colossal, like a sea. We passed Lake Tanganyika and are now over elephant country but too high to see without field glasses. We left a lot of people at Kampala. Amongst them was Lady Hall, wife of the Governor of Uganda, a charming lady whose company we were sorry to lose. She drove off in a government car, but waved heartily and looked sorry to leave us. We arrived at the Falls at about 2pm, I'm now going to concentrate on spotting an elephant!

(Mrs Adams, *née* Kirk, has since lost the final letter she sent home, but has kindly summarised the rest of her journey).

We parted company with the flying-boat and its crew to spend two nights at the posh Victoria Falls Hotel (where it was the rule men wear jacket and tie for dinner, despite the equatorial heat). I was enormously impressed with the Falls, but we never did see any elephants ... After the luxury of the Sunderland [actually a Solent] I was very much less than impressed when we boarded a tiny Dragon Rapide biplane. It appeared to have starched canvas wings, and no crew other than the pilot, who chatted to his passengers over his shoulder during the flight and told us a hair-raising tale about a baby being delivered on board the previous week. But he safely delivered us to Salisbury and the start of our new life ...

# 6

# THE PRINCESS FLYING BOAT

In July 1945 the Ministry of Supply invited tenders from the major UK aircraft manufacturers for designs for a very large flying boat type to meet what it then perceived as the future needs of BOAC. It was hoped that by applying the latest technological advances to the flying boat concept Britain could build on the success of the pre-war Empire flying boats and produce a design that would place BOAC at the forefront of the world's airlines. One of the companies submitting designs was Isle of Wight-based Saunders-Roe Ltd, which put forward a proposal for a gigantic machine with a 'double-bubble'-shaped hull able to accommodate up to 200 passengers in pressurised comfort on stages of more than 3,000 miles (including UK–New York non-stop) at a cruising speed of 350mph. The passengers would occupy the upper lobe of the fuselage, which would contain sleeper berths, powder rooms and a bar. The powerplant was originally intended to be the proposed Rolls-Royce Tweed engine, but after this project was cancelled the aircraft design was amended to incorporate no fewer than ten 3,200shp Bristol Proteus 600 turboprop engines. Eight of these were to be coupled in pairs driving contra-rotating propellers of 18ft 6in diameter, and the remaining two were to be mounted individually in the outermost of the three engine nacelles on each wing. Three examples of the aircraft were ordered by the Ministry of Supply on behalf of BOAC in May 1946 at a total contract price of £2.8 million. The flying boat type was originally going to be called the Dollar Princess, but this idea was soon dropped in favour of the designation SR.45 Princess.

At around the same time the Bristol Aeroplane Company was working on a rival design, the equally massive Brabazon landplane airliner. There

The massive Saunders-Roe SR.45 Princess in flight. (GKN Aerospace)

would obviously be insufficient funding for both types in the BOAC fleet of the future, and in a letter published in *Flight* magazine in August 1947 Captain T. Neville Stack set out what he considered to be the advantages of the flying boat option. He thought that the Brabazon design was pushing against the upper size limit for useful and economical operation by a landplane airliner. The dimensions of the runways and airport buildings necessary for safe and efficient operation would make such facilities extremely costly to construct. There was also the question of weather diversions to consider. How many airfields in the world, let alone in the UK, would be capable of accepting such an aircraft in emergency? The giant

The Saunders-Roe Princess in plan view, showing the six engine positions for the coupled turboprop powerplants. (GKN Aerospace)

flying boat was a much more practical alternative. There was no need for a technically difficult undercarriage to support the massive weight. The larger the hull was made the more seaworthy it would be. In the event of bad weather at its destination the flying boat had the whole ocean to alight upon. Rocket- or jet-powered assistance could be used to boost take-off performance, and in-flight refuelling could extend its range. In 1950 the Chairman of BOAC, Sir Miles Thomas, speaking about the future of the airline's services to Johannesburg, said that Princesses might be placed onto two-class flights to South Africa in about eight years' time. They should be capable of making the journey with just one stop at Lagos, and an extra stop at Lisbon could be incorporated if that proved commercially desirable. First-class sleeper berths could be provided on one deck, with the other given over to high-density seating.

The first prototype, registered as G-ALUN, was launched on 20 August 1952 and made its first flight two days later under the command of Geoffrey Tyson. There followed a series of test flights accumulating the required number of flight hours for the Princess to be demonstrated at the 1952 Farnborough Air Show. Saunders-Roe was planning on an initial production batch of twelve aircraft, to be constructed in the company's Columbine works. By that time the aircraft's development costs had escalated to £10.8 million, about half of which had been caused by the complexity of its coupled Bristol Proteus engines. Flight testing continued until June 1954. More than ninety flight hours were logged, in the course of which serious problems with the propeller gearboxes came to light. Work on the second and third prototypes was suspended while the Ministry, Saunders Roe, and Bristol tried to agree on the best way to install Bristol's new Orion turboprop engine in place of the Proteus powerplants. However, by then the concept and technology of the Princess had become dated, and BOAC had already ceased flying boat operations. The airline did carry out a survey of its former flying boat engineering base at Hythe, in case the Princess's powerplant problems could be solved, and agreed to reconsider the aircraft in that eventuality, but in truth it was no longer really interested.

During previous years, the British South American Airways Corporation (BSAAC) had examined the Princess design and had concluded that it would be able to operate the aircraft profitably on its two trunk routes to South America, using the natural marine locations along the way as flying boat bases. The airline had hopes of operating Princesses to Buenos Aires by 1953, but in July 1949 BSAAC was merged into BOAC and the scheme was subsequently dropped.

In late 1951 the government announced that 'circumstances have compelled a change in the civil plans, and the (Princess) flying boats are now to be completed for the Royal Air Force'. It was estimated that in trooping configuration a single Princess could transport in one year as many service personnel as nine conventional seagoing troopships. However, this scheme did not come to fruition either, and in early 1952 the Ministry of Supply decreed that in view of the continuing powerplant problems the second and third airframes should be 'cocooned' until the situation improved. By

An early view of the as-yet unpainted Saunders-Roe Princess above the clouds.
(GKN Aerospace)

February 1953 the work had been completed and the hulls were towed to Calshot for long-term storage. In 1954 it was announced that the entire Princess programme was to be terminated, and the only example to have made it into the air was also cocooned and stored at West Cowes. The three airframes were to remain cocooned and awaiting their uncertain future until the mid 1960s, when all three of them were finally broken up.

During their lifetime various alternative proposals for their use had been examined and eventually discarded. In 1952 Barry Aikman, chairman of the

Saunders-Roe Princess G-ALUN afloat off the Isle of Wight factory. In the foreground is the tail of another Princess under construction, and behind that the Saunders-Roe SR.A/1 jet fighter prototype. (GKN Aerospace)

British independent flying boat operator Aquila Airways, had expressed his interest in acquiring all three examples for use on trooping contracts and had offered the Ministry of Supply more than £1 million for each of them, only to have his offer declined. Also in 1952, Saunders-Roe had put forward a proposal for a jet-powered development of the Princess, to be called the Duchess. This would have been propelled by six De Havilland Ghost turbojet engines, enabling it to transport up to seventy-four passengers in luxury at 40,000ft and 500mph, but the project did not proceed beyond the design stage. In the late 1950s the US Navy considered using the airframes for part of its airborne nuclear reactor trials, but this idea also never came to fruition. Neither did a 1958 proposal to operate the three Princesses on services between Southampton and Rio de Janeiro, and also to the Great Lakes in Canada. As late as November 1963 Aero Spacelines Inc., the successful operator of the Pregnant Guppy conversion of a Boeing Stratocruiser landplane airliner, was reported to be in discussions with the NASA space

A night-time launch of the only Saunders-Roe Princess aircraft to fly, G-ALUN. (GKN Aerospace)

agency regarding a proposal to convert the first prototype Princess into a new 'Super Guppy' freighter for the transportation of the first stage of the USA's Saturn 5 rocket. This monster aircraft would have been powered by eight turbojet engines, giving it non-stop transcontinental range whilst carrying a 200,000lb payload. Aero Spacelines was sufficiently confident in the project to acquire the other two airframes as well, and in July 1965 all three were de-cocooned at Calshot and dismantled in preparation for shipment to the USA. However, Aero Spacelines then had second thoughts and decided to convert more Boeing Stratocruisers instead. In April 1967 the only Princess flying boat to have taken wing was towed up Southampton Water to meet its fate at a scrapyard on the River Itchen.

# 7

# AQUILA AIRWAYS

In 1948 Wing Commander Barry Aikman DFC decided to leave the RAF and use the expertise and experience gained during his time with No. 210 Flying Boat Squadron to set up his own flying boat airline. Aquila Airways was registered in May 1948 with a capital of £20,000 and the intention of operating the ageing Hythe-class Short Sunderlands that BOAC was in the process of retiring on ad hoc charter flights, round the world trips, and 'aerial cruises' to the Mediterranean. In July 1948 two Sunderlands were duly purchased from BOAC. One was intended for conversion to a freighter and the other was to retain its BOAC interior for the aerial cruise services. Southampton was selected as the airline's operating base as Aquila would be able to rent part of the terminal facilities and floating pontoons constructed for BOAC, and a recruiting drive for crews and ground staff began. The maintenance of the aircraft was contracted out to Air Service Training at nearby Hamble, whose slipway had originally been built for the aircraft manufacturer A. V. Roe during the First World War.

A starting date of 1 August 1948 for services out of Southampton was scheduled, but world events were to provide Aquila with the opportunity to earn some valuable extra revenue before then. Tensions between the Soviet Union and the Western allies were running high in the aftermath of the Second World War, and a Soviet blockade of road, rail and canal routes into Berlin through communist-held territory led to the Berlin Airlift, the Allied operation to supply the Berliners with food, fuel, oil, coal and other necessities entirely by air. Every suitable civilian aircraft was needed to supplement the military transport flights, and in August 1948 the two Aquila Airways Sunderlands began flying from the River Elbe at Finkenwerder

Aquila Airways Short Solent G-ANAJ *City of Funchal* moored off Madeira. (via author)

near Hamburg to Lake Havel in Berlin, carrying cargoes of meat, flour, and especially salt, for which the corrosion-proofed hulls of the flying boats proved ideal. The flights continued until December 1948, by which time the lake was expected to freeze over shortly, and so the Sunderlands were withdrawn from the airlift. By then the airline had acquired a third Sunderland from BOAC, and by late 1949 its fleet had grown to include twelve Sunderlands (some purchased for spares use only), and the Short Sandringham 5 G-AGKX. The company's plans for this expanded collection of aircraft now included the reconfiguring of two machines as fifty- to sixty-seaters for use on tourist-class charters and on emigrant flights to Australia. Aquila also had ambitions to operate scheduled passenger services from Southampton to the island of Madeira, which at that time possessed no land airport. The state-owned airlines BOAC and BEA (British European Airways) had a monopoly on UK scheduled services, but frequently permitted the independent airlines to operate services on their behalf under associate agreements. Aquila successfully applied to BEA for year-round services to Madeira under such an agreement, and on 24 March 1949 its

Sunderland G–AGEU *Hampshire* set off from Southampton on a combined route-proving/VIP inaugural flight to Madeira via Lisbon carrying seventeen invited guests, eight crew members and 110lb of mail. The airline had selected Funchal Bay as the alighting point for its scheduled services, but before landing there it flew the aircraft around the island to earmark possible alternative sites. When the Sunderland set down in Funchal Bay at 1402hrs on 25 March it became the first civilian airliner to land at Madeira, the island having been host to only a few military flying boats during the war years. The jetties and esplanades at Funchal were packed with curious residents, and when the crew later appeared in their uniforms for dinner at the Savoy Hotel they were applauded by the other diners as they entered. During the course of their two-day stay the crew were kept busy showing dignitaries over the aircraft and carrying some on sightseeing flights over Madeira and the neighbouring island of Porto Santo. At 1315hrs on 27 March the party departed for the journey back to Southampton via a fuel stop at Lisbon as Madeira possessed no refuelling facilities.

On 14 May 1949 Aquila Airways commenced regular fortnightly flights between Southampton and Funchal, and a weekly service linking Funchal with Lisbon. This latter service became very popular, as the alternative boat trip took some thirty-six hours. It was, however, mainly patronised by business travellers and civil servants as the fares were beyond the reach of most ordinary Madeirans. The Southampton–Funchal service was a success from the start, carrying more than 3,000 passengers on forty-two round trips during its first year. One of these passengers was the Right Honourable Winston Churchill, hurrying back to England from a painting holiday on Madeira on 12 January 1950 after a General Election had been called. Over the years other notable Aquila passengers were to include the entertainer Harry Secombe, the actress Constance Cummings, and a young Margaret Thatcher. From December 1951 Short Solents were introduced onto the route, with G–AKNU operating the first service by the type. This example was fitted out as a forty-one-seater, with its two decks linked by a spiral staircase. Most outbound passengers travelled by a particular train from Waterloo to Southampton Central station, where a motor coach and baggage van were waiting to take them to Berth 50 at the docks. Here, their baggage was weighed and their tickets, passports and visas (still required for travel to Madeira in the 1950s) were checked. They were then taken through to customs, and once the formalities had been completed they could relax in the bar and lounge in the Marine Terminal until it was time to board the flying boat. As soon as the aircraft was on its way to the take-off area further down Southampton Water the Aquila ground staff maintained a radio watch on the flying boat and its attendant launches until forty-five minutes or an hour had elapsed. Three types of launches were used by Aquila; a control pinnace (used as a floating control tower), a lead-in launch, and an uncovered work boat.

The Solents soon displaced the Sunderlands from the mainline route to Madeira, although the older type continued to be used on the Madeira–Lisbon link. Once the Southampton–Funchal service had become successfully established the owners of the Miramar Hotel in Funchal added a villa adjacent to the hotel for the exclusive use of visiting Aquila crews. In early 1952 Las Palmas was added to the route network, and the February/March 1952 flight schedule read:

The Aquila Airways Short Sunderland G-AGEU *Hampshire* moored off Funchal during the airline's inaugural service in 1949. (via author)

| TUE … | *Depart* Funchal 1000hrs (Sunderland). |
| | *Arrive* Lisbon 1515hrs. |
| WED … | *Depart* Lisbon 1130hrs (Sunderland). |
| | *Arrive* Las Palmas 1445hrs. |
| WED and SAT … | *Depart* Southampton 0045hrs (Solent). |
| | *Arrive* Funchal 0800hrs. |
| THURS and SUN … | *Depart* Funchal 0700hrs (Solent). |
| | *Arrive* Lisbon 1130hrs. |
| | *Depart* Lisbon 1230hrs. |
| | *Arrive* Southampton 1745hrs. |
| SAT … | *Depart* Funchal 1030hrs (Sunderland). |
| | *Arrive* Las Palmas 1230hrs. |
| | *Depart* Las Palmas 1430hrs. |
| | *Arrive* Funchal 1630hrs. |

Throughout its early years Aquila Airways tried with varying degrees of success to diversify its operations. During the summer of 1949 a series of holiday charter flights was operated from Falmouth to St Mary's in the Scilly Isles, and on 17 October that year Sunderland G-AGKY returned to Southampton from Foynes in Ireland after completing a short season of charter flights from there to Fatima in Portugal. Early in 1950 Aquila worked with Thomas Cook & Son to set up a programme of 'aerial cruises' around the Mediterranean, incorporating stopovers in Marseilles, Venice, Rome, Cyprus, Malta and Bordeaux. The fare for the 5,600-mile journey was set at £235, and the first departure was scheduled for 15 June that year, but in the event the series of flights had to be cancelled due to a lack of bookings.

Another attempt at diversification entailed an attempt to introduce scheduled flying boat services linking Southampton with Scotland during the summer of 1950. A round trip to Glasgow was scheduled for each Tuesday, with one to Edinburgh on Fridays. The fare to either city was to be £9 one-way, or just over £16 for a round trip, which was comparable to the first-class rail fare. On 1 June 1950 a route-proving flight with twenty-six invited guests and seven crew members on board was operated by Sunderland G-AGJN. The route was mostly overland, passing overhead Swindon, Oxford, Birmingham and Manchester before arrival at Edinburgh, where a water landing was made at the Leith Marine Airport, which had only been opened that day. After being welcomed by the Lord Provost of Edinburgh, the party flew on to Glasgow, alighting on the River Clyde near Greenock.

Scheduled services were due to commence during the first week in July, but these were destined never to take place, again because of a shortage of bookings. One venture that did prove successful was the reinstatement of the pre-war air link between Southampton and Jersey. On this service the Sunderlands were configured to carry up to twenty-nine passengers, with two round trips being operated each Saturday from 7 July 1950 until the end of the summer season. At Jersey the aircraft alighted in St Aubin's Bay, and the flights quickly proved very popular. By the autumn of 1950 BOAC had discontinued its flying boat services to South Africa, leaving Aquila as the only UK operator of the craft. Sensing an opportunity for expansion the airline applied to take over the former BOAC route, but permission was not forthcoming. Undeterred, Aquila continued to look for new routes, and on 17 May 1952 inaugurated scheduled services to Marseilles, again under a BEA associate agreement.

During May 1952 Aquila set out to lengthen the tourist season to the traditionally winter destination of Madeira by introducing a new low excursion fare for the summer months. The fare was valid for stays of up to twenty-one days commenced before 30 November, and at £59 10s 0d for the round trip offered a substantial reduction on the winter round trip fare of £89 2s 0d. As an additional incentive the airline also introduced a money-back guarantee, under which any passengers who experienced more than half an inch of rain during a holiday in July or August could claim back their full air fare plus a further £40 to cover hotel bills and other travel expenses. The Madeiran hoteliers also joined in the marketing effort by reducing their rates by as much as 25 per cent during the summer season. By taking advantage of these deals it was possible for British holidaymakers to enjoy full 'en pension' accommodation for the equivalent of as little as 18s 9d per day. These incentives proved very successful in attracting new business, and by August 1953 the summer passenger loads were almost double those of the previous year.

In 1952 there were also some notable non-scheduled flights. On 21 April Sunderland G-AGJN set off from Southampton for the Falkland Islands, on charter to the Falkland Islands Company. The aircraft finally arrived there on 28 July, after stops at Lisbon, Funchal, Cape Verde, Rio de Janeiro and Montevideo. In July and August 1952 the Summer Olympic Games were held in Finland, and Aquila operated charter flights to Helsinki in connection with these events. In August of that year the airline commenced a series of trooping flight charters, transporting servicemen and their families

The Aquila Airways Short Solent G-AKNU *Sydney* taxiing off Funchal. (via author)

to and from Singapore in a fifty-three-seater Short Solent. One of these passengers was Derek Sofe, who in October 1952 flew back to the UK with Aquila for demobilisation. He recalls that the same crew stayed with the aircraft throughout the whole journey, with stops being made at Karachi, Trincomalee, Goa, Bahrain, and Limassol. After Cyprus the next stop was scheduled to be at Malta, but for some reason the personnel there were unable to set out the necessary flarepath and so the aircraft was diverted to the French naval base at Bizerte before completing the last leg to Southampton. Aquila was to commence a second season of trooping flights on 16 January 1953, this time between Southampton and Freetown and Lagos in West Africa.

The first few months of 1953 saw several of the airline's flying boats involved in accidents, fortunately without serious injury to their occupants. On 21 January Sunderland G-AGJN dragged its moorings at Funchal, became holed on some rocks and eventually capsized. In Southampton a week or so later, Sunderland G-AGKY taxied out in preparation for a service to Madeira. The take-off run had to be abandoned and the aircraft developed a list to one side. According to a report in the *Times* newspaper, four female passengers clambered out onto the wing on the opposite side to try to keep the aircraft level until help arrived. In due course all twenty-seven passengers, the crew, and the baggage were safely taken aboard an Aquila launch and the Southampton fireboat. An attempt was made to tow the flying boat back to base, but during the journey it capsized. On 2 February a Sunderland en route from Lisbon to Funchal with thirty-six passengers had to turn back following an engine fire. A safe landing was accomplished at Lisbon, but the damage was such that the aircraft was deemed not repairable. Aquila had since 1950 been withdrawing and scrapping much of its Sunderland fleet, and these accidents left the airline with just one airworthy example, which continued to operate the 1953 schedules alongside the newer Solents. It was around this time that the airline's founder Barry Aikman first expressed an interest in acquiring the three giant Princess flying boats under construction. BOAC had lost interest in them and they were now being considered for completion as troop transports for the RAF. He submitted an offer in excess of £1 million per aircraft, but this was declined. The closure of BOAC's flying boat operation at Southampton had left Aquila in the unenviable position of having to maintain the facilities there single-handedly and entirely out of its own pocket. In an interview Mr Aikman outlined the problems his airline faced:

Madeira is perhaps exceptional. It is only because we can use facilities parallel to the shipping, and because the Portuguese charge us no landing fees, that we can keep our costs down. The other end of the route presents a very different picture. At Southampton we require more facilities because of the congestion in Southampton Water and because we operate there at night. Notwithstanding the fact that we provide and man our own facilities, the Harbour Board charges us a landing fee, the Docks and Inland Waterways Executive charges us a docking fee, and we have to use the port stevedores to handle our luggage. All this is very costly indeed. We use two radio-equipped control launches, one of which is stationed at the upwind end of the alighting area, and the other at the downwind end. At night we use five or more flare dinghies to mark out the alighting area between them. In addition to using all these, the Ministry of Civil Aviation still insists that we provide a fire float, although there is no case on record of a flying-boat catching fire on take-off or landing. Furthermore, if such a disaster did occur it is doubtful if it could offer any assistance. There is enough water around as it is. The only fire we have experienced at Southampton was when our fire float burst into flames and became a total loss.

Flying boat take-off runs were made at a full power setting and usually lasted between forty-five and fifty seconds. At Madeira the aircraft alighted at Funchal at dawn, when the sea was usually at its calmest. This necessitated a scheduled departure time from Southampton of 2300hrs, and meant that incoming flights usually arrived at Southampton after dark as well. On an 'Arrival Day' the first notification that an inbound service was on its way usually came in the form of a 'departure message' sent from Madeira and relayed via air traffic control at Hurn airport, Bournemouth. This gave details of the passenger load, mail and freight aboard, and was updated after the flight had left its transit stop at Lisbon. The aircraft crew eventually established direct radio contact with Berth 50 at Southampton and the control launch there about an hour before arrival. The experience of travelling by flying boat was described in a magazine article of the period thus:

> Because of the depth of hull necessary in a 'boat' there is real roominess, and the possibility of walking about and even climbing stairs during the flight. Because there is no pressurisation the windows can be big and numerous, with each one of them also being an emergency exit. And because of the need for watertight bulkheads there is none of the 'coach-tube', sardine-packed business. The Solent has two lower-deck passenger compartments, and aft of these is a promenade and bar with a spiral staircase leading to the upper deck. This compartment is probably the most comfortable from the noise and vibration point of view, although the promenade area is also good and there is nothing to complain about in the forward ground-floor compartments either. These become temporarily 'submarine' while the Solent is building up speed during the early part of the take-off run, until the aircraft gets up on its 'step'. Take-offs and landings are very great fun. I had long forgotten that slight

feeling of helplessness as the engines are run up and the propellers exercised with no brakes to hold the aircraft. All the warming-up and running-up can usually be done while the aircraft is taxiing out.

During the Coronation Naval Review of June 1953 Aquila was granted permission to operate a series of sightseeing flights overhead the fleet drawn up for Royal inspection. The flights were carried out at an altitude of 1,000ft within specially designated zones. That year Aquila carried around 6,000 passengers in total. By mid 1954 a second Solent had joined the fleet and two of the damaged Sunderlands returned to service, enabling Aquila to think once again about expansion and open a new route. On 20 May 1954 a VIP inaugural flight was operated to the Isle of Capri by Solent G-ANAJ. This was the first air service to Capri, with access to the island previously restricted to ferry boat journeys from Naples or Sorrento. On board the inaugural flight were thirty-nine invited guests, including the famous entertainer and Capri resident Gracie Fields and her husband. Fortnightly summer services began on 3 June 1954, routeing via Marseilles, where lunch was taken. On arrival at Capri the flying boats alighted in the harbour at Marina Grande. Including the ninety-minute stopover at Marseilles, the journey from Southampton took eight hours forty-five minutes. To begin with the service was all first class, with the fare set at £66 round trip. As had been the case at Madeira, the hoteliers on Capri helped to get the service established by offering reduced rates to visitors by air from the UK, and from 1 July Aquila was able to upgrade the service to weekly. In December 1954 three more Solents were acquired, these having previously served with the New Zealand airline TEAL. They would be needed the following summer, when newly approved services to Genoa and to Santa Margherita on the Italian Riviera would commence. In the course of its delivery flight from New Zealand the crew of Solent G-ANAJ took the opportunity to land at Genoa to gain experience of flying into this new destination. Summer services to Capri reopened on 2 June 1955, but with an all-economy-class cabin layout and a fare of £52 round trip. The new routes to Genoa and Santa Margherita quickly followed on 4 and 5 June respectively. For these, departure from Southampton was at 0300hrs, arriving at 0745hrs local time, thus allowing passengers the best part of an additional day on holiday.

The following year, 1956, was to be another eventful one for Aquila. Another new route, direct from Southampton to Las Palmas, was inaugurated on 8 January. In command of the inaugural flight was Captain James Broadbent, who was entering his twenty-first year of flying boat operations. Unfortunately his day was spoiled by the late arrival of the connecting train service from London that, coupled with adverse winds, delayed the departure of the first service until 2130hrs. A refuelling stop at Lisbon was required, and the aircraft eventually alighted at Las Palmas with the aid of a torch-lit flarepath at 0200hrs. The first daylight departures from Southampton were introduced for the summer 1956 season, but this innovation was offset by the suspension of the Capri service due to low bookings. Aquila said that it hoped to reintroduce flights to Capri the following summer as part of inclusive tour packages in conjunction with a holiday company. Other new services for 1956 were a summer service to Montreux, where the flying boat alighted on Lake Geneva, and the reinstatement of first-class travel to Genoa, with a dedicated weekly service, marketed as the Tigullian, which replaced the previous Saturday tourist-class flight. The Solent allocated to this new service had been reconfigured with an eighteen-seat passenger compartment, bar and galley on the upper deck. The lower deck was divided into three compartments accommodating a total of twenty-six passengers. Amidships was a toilet compartment with hot and cold water, a plug for an electric razor, and a separate drinking water supply. At the rear of the deck was a four-seat crew rest compartment. The capacity of the other Solents had been increased to fifty-eight tourist-class passengers by the removal of the cocktail bar and ladies' powder room.

Aquila was now operating an all-Solent fleet of four aircraft on ten services each week, but their annual utilisation of around 800 hours each was low, even by the standards of the time. They required constant maintenance, and anti-corrosion treatment after every service, and had become costly to operate. They were in need of replacement, but it was not at all clear how this could be achieved. In the meantime they soldiered on.

During the Suez Canal Crisis of 1956 Aquila used three Solents to fly naval personnel out of Malta, and then operated them on a shuttle service evacuating British civilian workers and their families from Fanara on the Great Bitter Lake in Egypt to Malta, from where landplanes took them onwards. During the year two of the Solents were damaged, fortunately without casualties. On 11 April G-ANYI suffered damage to its port float during a landing on rough water in the Bay of Genoa. In order to prevent the risk of capsizing the passengers were swiftly ordered out onto the starboard wing to balance the aircraft, before being transferred to small boats. The damaged float was repaired and the aircraft returned to service within forty-eight hours. On 26 September, at the very end of the tourist season, it was the turn of G-ANAJ to suffer damage. The aircraft was at Santa Margherita and should have operated a service to Southampton on the previous day, but the flight had been postponed because of rough seas. The conditions did not improve, and the Solent was blown from its moorings and onto the beach. As the service was over for the winter, the damage was not repaired, and a replacement Solent was acquired in time for the following

One of the Aquila Airways Short Solents, G-AKNU *Sydney*. (via Dave Thaxter)

season. The weather had been a continual cause of problems for Aquila, and the airline had imposed an operating limit of 4ft of swell for the operation of services. During the winter recess Aquila devoted more attention to the possibilities offered by inclusive tour flying, being granted a licence to operate package tour services to Majorca, and entering into an agreement with Club Mediterranee for charters, including flights from Marseilles to Palermo and Corfu.

During the summer of 1957 the scheduled services to Madeira continued to do well, and that year the airline's Solents carried almost one-third of the total number of tourists visiting the island. However, accidents continued to throw a shadow over the operations that year. During May G-ANYI struck a reef while taking off from Pollensa Bay in Majorca. On this occasion no injuries were sustained and the aircraft was repairable. However, on 15 November tragedy struck. G-AKNU was operating flight AQ101

A taxiing shot of Aquila Airways Short Solent G-ANAJ *City of Funchal*. (via Dave Thaxter)

Aquila Airways Short Solent G-ANAJ *City of Funchal* taxies past steep cliffs during the inaugural flight to Capri in 1954. (via Dave Thaxter)

from Southampton to Funchal and Las Palmas with fifty-eight occupants. Shortly after take-off the crew experienced engine problems and decided to turn back. They were unable to maintain height and the aircraft crashed at Shalcombe on the Isle of Wight. There were only thirteen survivors among the passengers, and all eight crew members perished. Aquila Airways ended 1957 with passenger numbers slightly up on the previous year, but the November crash had an impact on advance bookings for the following summer, and the company's problems were piling up. Services continued in 1958, but at a reduced frequency on many routes, and the operations were gradually being run down. In early summer the flying boats operated twice-weekly to Funchal via Lisbon and once-weekly to Genoa, but by July the Genoa route had been suspended. To add to the struggling airline's problems, abnormal sea conditions off Funchal made it impossible to alight there and the aircraft had to land off the northern coast of Madeira. There were no established handling facilities there, and so the turnarounds became very protracted. Finally, in July 1958, Aquila Airways announced that all of its operations would cease permanently at the end of the summer season. The main reasons cited were the lack of a suitable replacement for the elderly

The Aquila Airways Short Solent G-ANYI at Southampton. (via Dave Thaxter)

Solents, and increased competition from charter airlines operating more efficient landplanes into the Mediterranean resort areas. The three remaining Solents were put up for sale.

On 26 September 1958 Solent G-ANYI *Awateri* had the sad distinction of being the last passenger-carrying flying boat to depart Southampton when it set off from Berth 50 on the final Aquila service to Lisbon and Funchal. During the stopover in Madeira the aircraft's crew attended a farewell tea party at the British Consulate, followed by a special dinner at the Hotel Miramar. The return service was scheduled to arrive at Southampton in daylight for the convenience of the waiting media, but was delayed by engine problems. In the end, Captain Derek Weetman was eventually interviewed under floodlights after G-ANYI had arrived flying a 59ft 'paying-off' pennant from its mast. With its arrival, commercial flying boat operations at Southampton came to an end. Ownership of the three Solents was transferred to a Portuguese company called ARTOP for intended use on operations out of Lisbon under the company name of Aerovias Aquila. They were flown out to Lisbon but were destined never to enter service. Instead, ARTOP reopened the Lisbon–Funchal route with two Martin Mariner flying boats. One of the ARTOP pilots was former Aquila Airways Captain Jim Broadbent. He was in command of one of the Mariner aircraft on 9 November 1958 when it crashed shortly after take off with the loss of all on board. The Solents were beached and spent almost thirteen years slowly decaying on the banks of the River Tagus in Lisbon before they were finally broken up in 1971.

# 8

# AUSTRALIA AND THE SOUTH PACIFIC

On 18 January 1935 Qantas Empire Airways was established as a joint venture between the Australian airline Qantas and Britain's Imperial Airways, and given responsibility for the operation of the Singapore–Brisbane and return portions of the Empire Air Mail route to Australia. In 1938 three of the Short S.23 C-Class flying boats on order for Imperial Airways were transferred to Qantas Empire Airways (usually referred to as simply Qantas) for use on this service. The first of them, named *Coolangatta*, was delivered in early April 1938 and was followed shortly afterwards by another named *Cooee*. On 10 June they both landed at the marine base at Rose Bay, Sydney, also sometimes referred to as Sydney Water Airport. On the 26th of that month the Imperial Airways C-class flying boats *Camilla* and *Cordelia* set off from Southampton shortly after dawn, carrying 3 tons of mail and twenty passengers. Among the passengers were seven British and one Australian journalists, bound for Sydney on tickets paid for by Qantas. When the two aircraft reached Karachi *Camilla*'s passengers were transferred to *Cordelia* and the first aircraft returned to the UK as planned. On the evening of 3 July *Cordelia* arrived at Darwin, where her passengers were dismayed to find that hardly any preparations had been made for their arrival apart from the laying of a few buoys to mark the alighting area. No sooner had the flying boat been moored than it was boarded by immigration officers. The health certificates of the occupants were scrutinised and it was announced that three passengers and three of the crew had not been adequately vaccinated and additional injections must be administered before they could leave the aircraft. After two hours had elapsed the refuelling had been completed but the passengers and crew had still not been allowed to disembark. Eventually

An Ansett Airways Short Sandringham about to alight. (Ansett Australia)

a small boat was found to ferry them ashore in three batches to a small and inadequate customs shed. The journalists made clear their dissatisfaction with their treatment in the reports they filed for their newspapers. When their articles were published the repercussions made sure that when the next service arrived on 9 July the port officials had its occupants ashore within nine minutes, and the inspection of their luggage was carried out

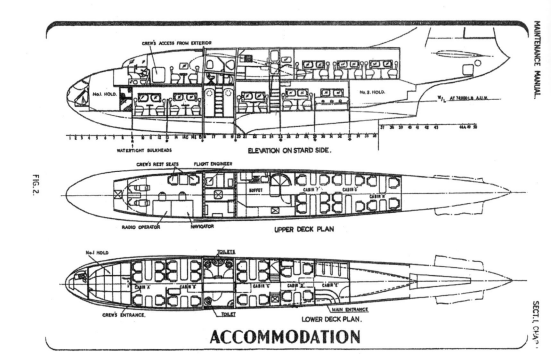

CREW'S ACCESS FROM EXTERIOR

No.I. HOLD.

No.3. HOLD.

W/L AT 78,000 LB A.U.W.

WATERTIGHT BULKHEADS

ELEVATION ON STARD SIDE.

FIG. 2.

CREW'S REST SEATS

FLIGHT ENGINEER

BUFFET

CABIN 'F'

CABIN 'G'

CABIN 'H'

RADIO OPERATOR

NAVIGATOR

UPPER DECK PLAN

No.I HOLD

TOILETS

CABIN 'A'

CABIN 'B'

CABIN 'C'

CABIN 'D'

CABIN 'E'

CREW'S ENTRANCE.

TOILET

MAIN ENTRANCE

LOWER DECK PLAN.

## ACCOMMODATION

A diagram of the interior layout of a TEAL Short Solent. (via author)

by customs officers in the more comfortable surroundings of the Dan Hotel. In the meantime, *Cordelia* had completed her journey to Sydney on 5 July, the date on which Captain Lynch-Blosse of Qantas commanded the inaugural Sydney–UK service as far as Singapore, where he handed over to an Imperial Airways crew. The first public scheduled service duly followed on 4 August 1938.

In 1939 the Qantas services from Sydney to Singapore travelled to Townsville via Brisbane and Gladstone on the first day. After a night stop they continued onwards via Karumba and Groote Eylandt to Darwin. After a dawn departure on the following day the passengers were flown across the Timor Sea to Koepang and Bima before the final night stop at Surabaya. They were up early again the next day for another dawn departure to Batavia and Klabat Bay before finally arriving at Singapore. In the course of their journey the passengers were kept well fed. Breakfast consisted of bacon and eggs, or sausages, or fish. For lunch, soup, chicken, and ham or a cutlet were

**Right:** A Qantas poster promoting the joint Qantas/Imperial Airways flying boat service between London and Sydney. (Qantas Heritage Collection)

**Far right:** A Qantas poster promoting the airline's UK–Australia Empire flying boat services. (Qantas Heritage Collection)

**Below:** A TEAL poster featuring one of its Short S.23 flying boats. (via author)

**Above:** A TEAL poster promoting the airline's Coral route and featuring a cutaway illustration of a Short Solent. (via author)

**Far left:** TEAL poster featuring a C-class flying boat. (via author)

**Left:** Aquila Airways luggage label. (Dave Thaxter)

Artist's impression of Qantas Short S.23 VH-ABA *Carpentaria* at her moorings. (Qantas Heritage Collection)

A cutaway diagram of a Pan American Airways Martin M-130. (via author)

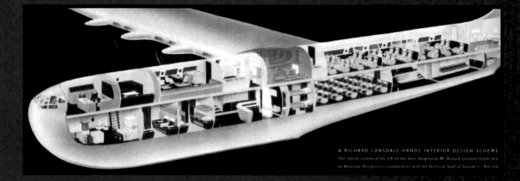

Artist's impression of a proposed interior layout for the Saunders-Roe Princess flying boat. (via author)

Artist's impression of the 'Honeymoon Suite' compartment at the rear of the Boeing 314s. (via author)

Ansett Short Sandringham VH-BRC *Beachcomber* ashore at the Rose Bay, Sydney base. (Ian McDonell collection)

Short Sandringham VH-BRF at Rose Bay, Sydney, in Antilles Air Boats livery after sale. (Stuart Bremner)

Ansett Short Sandringham VH-BRC on Lake Eucumbene in the Snowy Mountains during a charter flight. (Geoff Goodall)

The front end of Ansett Short Sandringham VH-BRC in November 1973, with the purser standing in the nose mooring hatch. (Geoff Goodall)

Short Sandringham VH-BRC in an old Ansett livery at Lord Howe Island, c. 1954. (Barrie Colledge collection)

View from cabin of Ansett Short Sandringham VH-BRF while taxiing at Lord Howe Island in July 1974. By then the scheduled service from Sydney had officially been terminated. (Geoff Goodall)

Shortly after a dawn departure from Lord Howe Island in Ansett Short Sandringham VH-BRF in July 1974, after the scheduled service had officially ceased. (Geoff Goodall)

An impressive sight as Ansett Short Sandringham VH-BRF takes off. (Stuart Bremner)

The French airline RAI used its Short Sandringham F-OBIP for services between Papeete and Bora Bora. (Ron Cuskelly collection via Queensland Air Museum)

The former Aerolineas Argentinas Short Sandringham LV-AHH at the Waterfront Rio de la Plata, Buenos Aires. (via Raul)

The amazing Boeing 314 full-size replica available for inspection at Foynes, Ireland. (Foynes Flying boat and Maritime Museum)

on the menu. Cheese and biscuits, tea and coffee were served with all meals. Smoking was permitted, but only in the aft compartment. Dinner was always taken ashore at the night stop location.

After an enforced break during the Second World War the service was reinstated on 12 May 1946 as part of the joint Qantas/BOAC Kangaroo route to London, this time using Hythe-class flying boats configured to carry twenty-one passengers. Passengers were supplied with literature describing the points of interest along the way:

> Leaving Rose Bay the route skirts the rich, sub-tropical coast, permitting enchanting views of the Great Barrier Reef. A refuelling stop is made at Bowen, a prosperous North Queensland town. You then proceed north-west across Queensland, the Gulf of Carpentaria, and Arnhem Land to Darwin. The next stage finds you over the Timor Sea and flying along the fascinating islands of the Netherlands East Indies, Surabaya-bound. Departure for Singapore leaves Java behind, with Sumatra on the port side and Borneo to starboard. From Singapore your aircraft is flown by BOAC personnel. You depart early next morning en route to Rangoon along the interesting Malayan Peninsular. From Rangoon the flying-boat turns north-west over the head of the Bay of Bengal to Calcutta, and on across India to Karachi. On the following day stops are made at Bahrain and Basra, and you fly high across the sandy wastes of Saudi Arabia to Cairo. Then over the Libyan desert and the Mediterranean to Augusta in Sicily, onto Marseilles, and cross France to alight in southern England.

On 17 November 1945, at the request of the governments of Australia and New Zealand, Qantas opened a route linking Sydney with Suva in Fiji via Noumea in New Caledonia. This was the last route to be opened using C-class flying boats, and as *Coriolanus* was the last operational example it was this aircraft that flew the inaugural service and also the final service by the type, alighting at Rose Bay, Sydney, from Noumea on 20 December 1947. After the aircraft's retirement Captain Crowther of Qantas offered to purchase her for £200, but had his offer rejected and she was eventually scrapped. By 1947 more than 270 people were employed at the Rose Bay base. During that year another flying boat route, this time to Norfolk Island, was opened. Initially, Catalina aircraft were used on this route and on a fortnightly service to Noumea and Suva, but in 1950 these machines were superceded by two Short Sandringhams that Qantas had purchased from

A TEAL advertisement for its Short Solent flying-boat services from New Zealand to Fiji and Australia. (via author)

the New Zealand airline Tasman Empire Airways Ltd, usually abbreviated to TEAL. One of them, registered VH–BRC, went into storage at first while VH–BRD was used for twice-weekly services out of Brisbane to Townsville, Cairns, Lindeman Island, Daydream Island, and the South Molle Islands. However, during the night of 10/11 September 1952 this aircraft was struck by a boat at her moorings and badly damaged, and VH–BRC was brought out of storage to continue the services. The Qantas flying boat operations at Brisbane had been using the Hamilton Reach stretch of the Brisbane River, but this had become congested with shipping movements and could not be used after dark, so in 1953 the services were transferred to Redland Bay, the nearest suitable alternative site for a marine airport. The Qantas service from Rose Bay to Noumea and Fiji was scheduled to alight at Redland Bay at around 2300hrs with the aid of a powerful searchlight. During the two-hour refuelling stop there, passengers in transit were able to come ashore and take refreshment at the Redland Bay Hotel. Another stop was made at Noumea, where breakfast was served ashore, and then it was all back on board for the five-hour leg to Fiji. Flying boat activity at Redland Bay reached its peak in July 1953 when 105 commercial movements passed through. The Sandringhams were also utilised on services to other island destinations, and Qantas flying boat operations to New Guinea were to continue until 1960.

On 2 April 1937 the British, Australian and New Zealand governments reached agreement in principle on the operation of joint air services across the Tasman Sea between Australia and New Zealand, operated by TEAL. Two C-class Empire flying boats were ordered for TEAL to use, and at 1430hrs on 28 August 1939 the first one, ZK-AMA *Aotearoa*, arrived at Auckland from Sydney on the last leg of its long delivery flight. By then,

Mechanics Bay in Auckland, with TEAL Short S.30 Empire flying-boats ZK-AMA and ZK-AMC on the water with two RNZAF Short Sunderlands. (State Library of South Australia)

however, most of the UK aircraft production was for military use, and it was considered impractical to try to launch trans-Tasman services with just a single aircraft, so *Aotearoa* spent several months engaged on route-proving flights across the Tasman Sea and out across the Pacific to Noumea, Suva, Tonga and Western Samoa. Eventually, in March 1940, the second TEAL machine, ZK-AMC *Awarua*, set off from Poole on her delivery flight. On board were six passengers. These were mostly TEAL staff travelling on duty, but also aboard was Miss Ame Harrison, the first fare-paying passenger from England to New Zealand. During 1940 one of the TEAL machines was used to transport dignitaries to the New Zealand Centennial Exhibition in Wellington. Here, the alighting point was at Evans Bay, where a temporary passenger terminal was improvised out of the roadside parking garages along Evans Bay Parade. A more substantial terminal was to be constructed on

Trans-Oceanic Airways Short Sunderland VH-AKO, with a passenger launch alongside. (Qantas Heritage Collection)

TEAL Short Sandringham ZK-AMB *Tasman* being loaded with parcels at Mechanics Bay, Auckland, in May 1949. (Alexander Turnbull Library, Wellington)

reclaimed land there in 1951, and after flying boat services had ceased the site later became the home of a local yachting club.

On 13 April 1940 *Aotearoa* inaugurated weekly scheduled services on the 1,370-mile journey across the Tasman, carrying nine passengers and 41,000 letters from Auckland to Sydney. When the first service in the opposite direction set off on 2 May, the final link in the Empire Air Mail Scheme had been forged. At 14,277 miles from Auckland to Poole, this became the world's longest air route. The passenger capacity was initially restricted to fifteen, but was later increased. Passengers arriving at Auckland were able to connect with Pan American Airways services to Honolulu and San Francisco

FLYING BOATS

until the Japanese attack on Pearl Harbor in 1941 brought about the suspension of all Pan American flights west of Hawaii. On 18 August 1940, in the course of a trans–Tasman service to Auckland, TEAL's *Awarua* passed within 40 miles of Pan American's *California Clipper*, out of Auckland for San Francisco. Although the two crews exchanged radio messages they were unable to establish visual contact. On 21 May 1944, for the first time, the

TEAL Short Sandringham ZK-AMB *Tasman* riding 'on the step' at Waitemata Harbour, Auckland, around 1949. (R.N. Smith Collection, copyright to aussieairliners.org)

two TEAL flying boats arrived at Auckland on the same day. Unfavourable weather conditions on previous days had resulted in the doubling up of the service, with the two aircraft landing within twenty minutes. *Aotearoa* was to operate the 1,000th trans-Tasman service on 19 June 1945. During the flight from Sydney to Auckland each of the eighteen passengers was presented with a commemorative certificate by the captain, Oscar Garden. In the five years since the service was inaugurated the two flying boats had maintained the operation without injury to passengers or loss or damage to cargo or mail. By the end of the Second World War Britain had withdrawn its financial interest in the airline and TEAL was owned solely by the governments of Australia and New Zealand.

In 1946 the frequency of the Auckland–Sydney service was increased to four round trips each week. The C-class flying boats were nearing the end of their service lives, and on 2 July 1946 the first of four Short Sandringham 4s ordered to replace them was launched at the Belfast works. The Sandringhams were conversions of surplus RAF Short Sunderland airframes. The process included the removal of their armament, the fitting of large passenger windows, the replacement of the windscreens with new curved versions, the replacement of the bow and tail sections with streamlined fittings, the installation of thirty seats on the lower deck, and the modification of an aft upper cabin to serve as a bar and galley. Power was provided by four Pratt & Whitney Twin Wasp engines. The Sandringhams were initially going to be advertised by TEAL as the Dominion class, but this was later changed to the Tasman class. The type entered service on the Auckland (Mechanics Bay)–Sydney (Rose Bay) route in December 1946, permitting the retirement of the two C-class machines. *Awarua* was withdrawn on 16 June 1947, and *Aotearoa* after the completion of its 442nd trans-Tasman service on 29 October that year. Both aircraft were eventually broken up, but before succumbing *Aotearoa* served ashore as a tearoom at Mechanics Bay from June 1948 until October 1950.

The Sandringhams' engines proved prone to overheating on the long trans-Tasman legs. On 3 December 1947 ZK-AME *New Zealand* encountered just such a problem. Her crew managed to nurse her safely back to Sydney, but only after the flying boat had been lightened by the jettisoning of the mail and cargo. In an effort to cure the problem the Sandringhams were withdrawn for a thorough overhaul in February 1948. They duly returned to service, but were withdrawn permanently in 1949. The more modern Short Solent had been selected as their replacement, but until this type could be

TEAL Short Sandringham ZK-AMD *Australia* at Mechanics Bay, Auckland, in January 1948.
(Alexander Turnbull Library Wellington)

delivered the trans–Tasman route had to be maintained by chartered Douglas
DC-4 landplanes.

TEAL was not the only New Zealand airline to operate flying boat services
out of Auckland. On New Year's Day 1949 the New Zealand National
Airways Corporation (NZNAC) had inaugurated weekly flights between
Auckland, Suva, and Labasa, Fiji, using former Royal New Zealand Air Force
Short Sunderlands. They also began services from Auckland and Wellington
to the New Zealand-owned Chatham Islands, but abandoned this route in
March 1950, leaving the remote island location without air links until TEAL
reopened services with Short Solents. The first TEAL Solent 4, registered
ZK–AML, was named *Aotearoa II* by HRH Princess Elizabeth in a ceremony

at the Belfast works on 26 May 1949, and the type entered service on the Auckland–Sydney route at the end of that year. On 6 June 1950 TEAL took over the service to Suva and Labasa from NZNAC, and on 3 October introduced Solents onto flights linking Wellington and Sydney. Each week, Sydney was served by five flights from Auckland and three from Wellington.

The Solent 4 was a variant produced specifically for the TEAL network of long stages, and was a vast improvement on the earlier Solent 2s and 3s. Its four 2,040hp Bristol Hercules 733 engines gave it an economical cruising speed of 230mph at an altitude of 10,750ft, and a range of 2,330 miles. The take-off run of 900yd or so was usually accomplished in around twenty-six seconds. Like its earlier models, the Solent 4 was unpressurised. Accommodation was provided for forty-five passengers and was divided into seven compartments on the two decks, linked by a spiral staircase. The reclining seats were upholstered in deep blue fabric with cream-coloured antimacassars and were equipped with 'winged' headrests, armrests with ashtrays, folding tables for meals and card games, overhead reading lights, and warm/cool fresh air louvres. The four seats forward of the main entrance foyer could be converted into twin bunks for the transportation of sick passengers, and bassinets for infants could also be fitted. Elsewhere in the cabin were four toilets, a galley and a crew rest compartment. Luggage and freight were stowed in the forward and aft cargo holds. On the spacious flight deck sat the captain, first officer, radio officer, and flight engineer. The first officer was also responsible for the navigation of the aircraft, as all TEAL pilots were also required to hold a first-class navigator's licence. The passengers were attended to by a senior flight steward, a flight steward, and a flight hostess.

At the end of 1951 a new £20,000 marine aircraft terminal building was opened at Evans Bay, Wellington, with the first scheduled service from here being operated by ZK-AMN on the last day of that year. The first service on TEAL's Coral route to Tahiti via Fiji set off from Auckland on 27 December 1951, operated by Solent ZK-AMQ *Aparima*. The name for the service had been the winning entry in a TEAL staff competition, and had been submitted by one of the airline's stewards.

The route was operated once-monthly at first, but by May 1952 it had been upgraded to fortnightly. A typical journey along the Coral route would begin with departure from Mechanics Bay, Auckland, in the morning for a seven-and-a-half-hour flight to the Laucala Bay Marine Air Base at Suva, Fiji. After alighting there the passengers would be taken ashore and

TEAL Short Sandringham ZK-AMD *Australia* taking off from Waitemata Harbour, Auckland, in September 1946. (Alexander Turnbull Library Wellington)

there on the 15th brought to an end the last scheduled flying boat service in the world.

In Australia, in addition to Qantas, several other flying boat operators were active in the 1950s. Barrier Reef Airways had been founded in Queensland by Captain Stewart Middlemiss and Captain Poulson back in 1946. Two Catalina flying boats were used initially, on twice-weekly services between Brisbane and Heron Island and between Brisbane and Gladstone, and a weekly schedule linking Brisbane with Lindeman Island, Daydream Island, and the South Molle Islands. In 1950 two Short Sandringhams were acquired from TEAL, overhauled, and converted to carry forty-one

TEAL Short Sandringham ZK-AME *New Zealand* gets airborne from Waitemata Harbour, Auckland, around 1948. (R.N. Smith Collection, copyright to aussieairliners.org)

passengers. One of these, registered VH-BRC and named *Coral Clipper*, inaugurated Sandringham services on the Brisbane–Lindeman Island–Daydream Island route on 23 May 1950. Sandringham services to Hayman Island commenced on 2 July that year. By then, Barrier Reef Airways had merged with Ansett Airways in April 1950. Services under the Barrier Reef Airways name continued until 12 November 1950, after which the airline was fully absorbed into Ansett.

In February 1947 Captain Brian Monckton set up Trans-Oceanic Airways, with the intention of acquiring one or two surplus Short Sunderlands from the Royal Australian Air Force as his initial equipment. In the event, he was obliged to enter into an agreement to purchase a package of five aircraft plus spare engines for a total price of £10,000. Two of these aircraft were scrapped, but the other three entered service, and in May 1947 were joined by the airline's first Short Sandringham. Trans-Oceanic was eventually to operate three examples of this type, configured to carry thirty-eight passengers. In February 1949 the airline was still operating the Sunderlands in a thirty-six-seat layout on regular services between Sydney (Rose Bay) and the Solomon Islands, the New Hebrides, and New Caledonia. During that month the Sunderland *Australia* also made its first visit to Lord Howe Island, on an emergency food flight. Trans-Oceanic also built up a network of services linking Sydney with Hobart, Grafton, Taree, and Port Macquarie on the coast of New South Wales. In April 1950 a Trans-Oceanic Sandringham alighted on the Clarence River at Grafton with a load of thirty-three passengers and 8,500lb of mail, at that time the greatest weight of mail carried by a single aircraft in Australia. These internal flights were taken over by the Sandringhams of Qantas that year, but by then Trans-Oceanic was also operating to Fiji and was able to report a 50 per cent increase in traffic over the previous year. Two Short Solent 2s were purchased from BOAC to cope with the expansion, and on 25 January 1951 the first of these, now re-registered as VH-TOA, set off on its delivery flight after overhaul at Belfast. One of the many stops was at Marseilles, where a party of twenty-nine German technicians bound for Brisbane joined the aircraft. On 26 January the aircraft was prepared for the next leg to Malta, but whilst taxiing for take-off it suddenly sank, with the loss of one life. The second Solent arrived safely in Australia in April 1951 and was registered there as VH-TOB. Later in the year two further Solents were acquired from BOAC, and the type first appeared on the Sydney–Hobart route in a forty-four-seat configuration.

Throughout 1951 Trans-Oceanic Solents and Sandringhams flew this route six times each week, also operating twice-weekly from Sydney to Lord Howe Island and from Sydney to Grafton, and on the once-weekly Chieftain service from Sydney to Brisbane and Port Moresby. However, the airline's reputation was marred by several non-fatal accidents that year and in the one to follow. In October 1951 VH-TOC collided with a dredger during its take-off run on the Brisbane River and was declared a total loss. On 11 February 1952 VH-TOB lost a propeller and its reduction gear in the course of a Sydney–Hobart service. The Solent was landed safely, but the same aircraft was in trouble again on 22 March when it struck a small cargo vessel at the beginning of a Brisbane–Port Moresby service. This time it was out of action for four weeks.

In April 1953 Trans-Oceanic Airways ceased operations and went into
voluntary liquidation. By then, its founder, Bryan Monckton, had left the
company and moved on to a new venture. During 1952 he had secured
financial backing to set up South Pacific Air Lines. In 1953 the new
company obtained Civil Aeronautics Board recommendation for a direct
Honolulu–Tahiti service. It was the first airline to propose operating such
a service on a regular basis, and planned to use two forty-seat Short Solents
on one round trip each week. The one-way journey would take between
fourteen and seventeen hours, including a proposed refuelling stop at
Christmas Island in the Pacific. Services would hopefully commence

TEAL Short Sandringham ZK-AME *New Zealand* at Laucala Bay, at Suva, Fiji, in May 1947.
(Alexander Turnbull Library Wellington)

transported by limousine to the Grand Pacific Hotel on the waterfront for afternoon tea. They would then have time for a nap before dinner preceded by pink gins and a night's sleep ashore. On the next day the flying boat would transport them on the three-hour journey to Western Samoa. Here they would alight in the lagoon and be transported to Aggie Grey's Hotel in Apia for another night stop. The next morning they would be up early for the flight to Aitutaki in the Cook Islands, where the airline had erected some native-style huts in tropical surroundings. After the Solent had been moored in Akaiami Bay, a TEAL launch would ferry the passengers to the landing stage, where they would be welcomed and presented with the traditional leis, garlands of sweet-smelling flowers. TEAL had also constructed a small fuel depot at Aitutaki, and while fuel was pumped into the aircraft from a barge the passengers and crew could make the most of the two- to three-hour stopover by swimming from the sandy beach or relaxing in the small TEAL guesthouse. Then it was all back aboard again for the final leg to Papeete in Tahiti. From March 1953 an additional stop at Tonga was added. The Coral route proved especially popular with American tourists, who could fly by landplane from San Francisco to Fiji to connect with the flying boat. Many famous passengers passed through Aitutaki en route to Tahiti, including the movie star Marlon Brando and Crown Prince Tupou of Tonga, the son of Queen Salote. Because of his great girth, whenever he travelled TEAL installed a specially large seat at the rear of the cabin for his use. By the end of 1952, with the exception of a DC-4 landplane link between Christchurch and Melbourne, the entire TEAL route network was being operated by an expanded fleet of five Solents. In December 1953 the Solent ZK-AML *Aotearoa III* transported HM Queen Elizabeth II and the Duke of Edinburgh on a section of their Royal Tour of the Pacific islands and New Zealand. From Laucala Bay in Fiji they flew to Lautoka, where they went ashore before returning to Fiji later that day. At 0900hrs on 19 December they boarded the Solent again for a three-hour flight to Nukualofa in Tonga, from where they continued their itinerary by ship.

In June 1954 the Solents were displaced from the trans-Tasman services by landplanes. Four of them were withdrawn completely, but ZK-AMO *Aranui* continued to serve on the Coral route to Papeete until 1960. The completion of a new land airport on Tahiti in 1959 had spelt the beginning of the end of the flying boat service, and on 14 September 1960 ZK-AMO departed Lauthala Bay in Fiji on its return journey to Auckland. Its arrival

in 1956, and an extension to Fiji would later be added. Three Solents were acquired, two of them former Trans-Oceanic aircraft and the other ex-Aquila Airways. By May 1956 all three aircraft had been delivered. One of the former Trans-Oceanic examples was overhauled, re-registered as N9964F and, given the name *Isle of Tahiti*, was used for a proving flight from Honolulu to Christmas Island and Papeete and back in December 1958, but at this point the airline's plans began to unravel. Christmas Island was under the jurisdiction of the British government, who had designs on using it for hydrogen bomb testing and objected to its proposed use as a staging post. Further licensing problems were encountered, and eventually South Pacific Air Lines collapsed before it could operate a single service.

Much more successful was the Australian operator Ansett Flying boat Services, formed in April 1950 when Barrier Reef Airways merged with Ansett Airways. The airline's initial fleet comprised two Barrier Reef Airways Catalina flying boats and two Short Sandringhams acquired from the New Zealand airline TEAL. These were used to continue the operations to the Barrier Reef area, including Hayman Island, and to extend the Ansett network northwards to Townsville and Cairns. In 1951 services between Southport (Broadwater) and Sydney were added, and further expansion came in 1953 when Ansett Flying boat Services purchased the assets of the defunct Trans Oceanic Airways. These included its Sunderland aircraft, its base at Rose Bay, and licences for scheduled services from Sydney to Lord Howe Island, Grafton, and Hobart. In January 1953 the Catalina VH-BRA was used to carry Mr R.M. Ansett and Captain Middlemiss on a proving flight to Tahiti, but these aircraft were reaching the end of their useful lives, and at the conclusion of this flight both Catalinas were retired. In March 1953 Ansett Flying boat Services transferred its headquarters from Brisbane to the newly acquired premises at Rose Bay, Sydney, which was to become one of the last fully equipped flying boat bases in the world.

The airline's route network now covered an area from Hobart to Cairns and included services to Grafton, Southport and Hayman Island, and also the Sydney–Lord Howe Island route. Lord Howe Island is situated in the Pacific Ocean, 420 nautical miles north-east of Sydney. It is 7 miles long by 1½ miles wide and is renowned for its magnificent scenery. The Sandringhams used on the service covered the distance in three to four hours, depending on the winds, at a cruising speed of 128–138 knots. On arrival the flying boats would alight on a lagoon situated a mile north

TEAL Short Sandringham ZK-AMH *Auckland* being returned to the water from the TEAL
slipway at Mechanics Bay, Auckland, in March 1950. (Alexander Turnbull Library Wellington)

of the twin peaks of Mount Gower and Mount Lidgbird. The return leg
departed later the same day, landing at Sydney after dark with the aid of
a flarepath of battery-powered lamps. A passenger on a Rose Bay–Lord
Howe Island service recorded his impressions:

The time would come to board, and it was down the ramp and onto the pontoon. The steward would welcome you aboard, having to take your arm as it was quite a step across into the aircraft. So it was all very personal, right from the set off ... There were, of course, meals as appropriate, and they were beautiful meals. Salads, sometimes a hot meal, but mostly salads. Sweets, drinks with bar service, naturally. Time didn't matter. Your holiday on Lord Howe Island started and finished at Rose Bay. It was a continuous part of a marvellous experience ... On board the flying-boat you almost felt like you were a member of the crew. Anyone could pop up to the flightdeck if they were interested. It made you feel that you were part of an adventure, part of the aircraft ... Flying in, you could usually see the island from 25 to 30 miles out. You would usually circle the island while the crew took a look at the lagoon. It was like a dream. And then to land on the lagoon ... It was like coming up to a sheet of glass. You could see the bottom of the lagoon, the coral. Quite magnificent. Then of course you taxied the length of the lagoon and came to the mooring. Local boats would come out and take you ashore from the flying-boat.

TEAL Short Solent ZK-AML *Aotearoa II* in the later livery on the hard-standing at Mechanics Bay, Auckland around 1952. (R.N. Smith Collection, copyright to aussieairliners.org)

TEAL Short Solent ZK-AMM with its engine cowlings open at Mechanics Bay, Auckland, in March 1950. (Alexander Turnbull Library Wellington)

TEAL Short Solent ZK-AMM moored at Papeete, Tahiti, in October 1952. (Alexander Turnbull Library Wellington)

On 10 September 1952 Sandringham VH-BRD *Princess of Cairns* was at its moorings on the Brisbane River when it was struck by a fishing vessel during the night and sank. It was later salvaged after being purchased for conversion to a nightclub at Coolangatta, but while under tow in an unseaworthy state it capsized again. This time it was not recovered, and was replaced by a former Qantas example. As well as maintaining the schedules the Sandringhams were also used for some charter work, including fishing trips to Lake Eucumbene in the Snowy Mountains, and 'flying boat cruises' to destinations such as Tahiti.

TEAL Short Solent ZK-AMM at full power for take-off from Waitemata Harbour, Auckland, in March 1950. (Alexander Turnbull Library Wellington)

From 1954 onwards the scheduled flying boat services were slowly run down. The stops at Townsville and Cairns were deleted and the flying boats then just operated Sydney–Brisbane–Hayman Island. In 1957 the routes to Tasmania were transferred to a new parent company, Ansett ANA, and in March 1958 Ansett Flying boat Services was placed under the control of another Ansett company, Airlines of New South Wales, although it retained its own operating identity. By 1959 the only flying boat services still operating were those between Sydney and Lord Howe Island and the occasional charter flight. The Lord Howe Island services were to continue throughout the 1960s, despite the loss of VH-BRE *Pacific Chieftain*. On 3 July 1963 she was on the first leg of an 8,500-mile charter cruise around

TEAL Short Solent ZK-AMN *Awatere* undergoes engine servicing at Evans Bay, Wellington, in October 1950. (Evening Post Newspapers image)

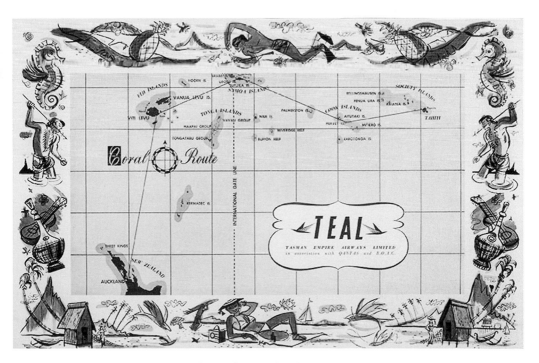

A TEAL map of the airline's Coral route from Auckland to Tahiti. (via author)

the islands of the South Pacific when she broke free from her moorings at Lord Howe Island during a violent storm, capsized and was damaged beyond repair. After being stripped of all usable fittings she was sunk outside the reef. A Sunderland V was purchased from the Royal New Zealand Air Force as a replacement in December 1963. This was converted to a

Contemporary travel fashions are shown off on the balcony of the flying-boat terminal at Rose Bay, Sydney. (Qantas Heritage Collection)

forty-two-seat civilian configuration (although not to full Sandringham specification) by Ansett at the Rose Bay base, registered as VH-BRF, and given the name *Islander*.

During the early 1970s the two Ansett flying boats were still carrying around 5,000 passengers between them each year. The services to Lord Howe Island were being subsidised by the Australian government, and were being hampered by the many operating restrictions placed upon them. By 1972 the flights out of the busy Sydney Harbour were only continuing under sufferance, with none at all permitted at weekends. The departure times from Sydney were governed by the tide states as well as the forecast weather at Lord Howe Island. Operations into the lagoon here were restricted to a 'window' of from two hours before high tide to two hours after, and at certain times of year the area was subjected to severe tropical storms. There were no refuelling facilities on the island, and so the aircraft always had to depart Sydney with enough fuel for the round trip. Towards the end of the year Sir Reginald Ansett, chairman and managing director of Ansett Transport Industries, issued a statement warning that Lord Howe Island could lose its air service within six months:

> These aircraft are reaching the end of their operational life. They are well maintained to the highest standards, but should have no place in Australian civil aviation ... An airstrip has to be built, and quickly ... The company has investigated all available flying-boats, amphibians, and short take-off and landing aircraft, and there is no doubt that the most satisfactory service can be provided with a Fokker Friendship.

During 1973 the flying boat services received AUD$170,000 in federal government subsidies, but by then a land airstrip was under construction on Lord Howe Island and it was clear that the end was in sight for the flying boats. The last official scheduled service was operated from the island to Sydney on 31 May 1974 by VH-BRC *Beachcomber*, but until the airstrip was fully operational the flying boats continued to operate 'facility flights' for the benefit of the islanders. On 8 June 1974 *Beachcomber* was chartered by the Australian Department of Environment and Conversation to transport a group of officials out to Lord Howe Island to examine the impact the new airstrip was having on the natural beauty of the island. While they were there the other flying boat, *Islander*, was due to depart Sydney on 17 June on delivery to the purchaser of the two aircraft, Antilles Air

The famous signpost at the Rose Bay flying-boat terminal, showing the route mileages to points in the Empire. (Qantas Heritage Collection)

Boats, in the Virgin Islands. However, these plans were disrupted on 9 June when *Beachcomber* broke free from her moorings on Lord Howe Island in an 80-knot gale and ran ashore onto the beach during the night. A team of sheet metal workers was flown out to the island and within three weeks had carried out temporary repairs to the severely damaged aircraft, which was then ferried to Rose Bay for more work to be done. *Islander*'s delivery flight had to be postponed, and she was sent out to Lord Howe Island to fly the charter group back to Sydney. On 10 September 1974 the now fully restored VH-BRC *Beachcomber* operated the final flying boat service from Lord Howe Island to Sydney. The Ansett base at Rose Bay, Sydney, was finally closed down in 1977.

In 1954 Captain P.G. Taylor, a former director of Trans-Oceanic Airways, travelled to England to take possession of the Short Sandringham 7 aircraft

Aerial view of the flying-boat terminal at Rose Bay, Sydney, under construction, with two Short S.23 aircraft moored offshore. (Qantas Heritage Collection)

The flying-boat terminal at Rose Bay, Sydney, with a tender alongside and the tail of a TEAL Empire flying-boat visible in the background. (Qantas Heritage Collection)

G-AKCO, which he had bought from the aircraft dealer W.S. Shackleton for £20,000. This aircraft had previously served with BOAC on services between Bermuda and the USA, and he had ambitions to use it for 'aerial cruises' from Sydney to 'the fabulous and beautiful islands in the South Pacific'. Each year he intended to offer around ten such trips on a variety of routeings taking in such holiday destinations as Fiji, Samoa, Tonga, and the Great Barrier Reef. To this end the Sandringham was furnished to accommodate thirty passengers in a luxurious interior containing five compartments, a bar, lounge and galley. Whilst waiting for the work to be completed he took the opportunity to sell places on the aircraft's delivery flight to Australia via Madeira, the South Atlantic, the Caribbean, California, and several Pacific islands. A maximum of twenty-five passengers were to be looked after by two flight attendants, and the fare for the one-way journey was set at £850. In due course the aircraft arrived safely in Australia, and was given the registration VH-APG and the name *Frigate Bird III*. The aerial cruises operated until May 1958. The Sandringham was then sold to the French air operator Regie Aerienne

Interinsulaire (RAI), and Captain Taylor commanded its delivery flight to Tahiti.

At that period in time the area of French Polynesia had no landplane links between its scattered islands. Seaplane flights had commenced at the start of the 1950s, and in 1953 two Catalina flying boats were acquired by Transports Aerienne Interinsulaire (TAI), a commercial division of the Regie Aerienne Interinsulaire (RAI) that operated for the Department of Public Works and Transport. A network of links between the islands was built up and in 1955 services in the Austral Archipelago were inaugurated with the opening of routes to Tubuai and Raivavae. In early 1958 TAI took a controlling interest in RAI and amended that organisation's name to Reseau Aerien Interinsulaire, which roughly translates as Inter-Island Aviation Network. In April of that year services connecting the airline's base at Papeete to Huahine, Raitea, and Bora Bora commenced. To cope with this expansion Captain P.G. Taylor's Short Sandringham 7 *Frigate Bird III* was purchased and re-registered as F-OBIP. It was placed into RAI service on 15 October 1958, providing the landplane services arriving at Bora Bora with connections to Papeete, which at that time had no land runway. RAI equipped it with accommodation for forty-five passengers, and it also gained a secondary role, being on call for air-sea rescue and casualty evacuation duties during emergencies. The Bora Bora to Papeete services were to continue until 20 September 1960, ten days before a new land airport was opened at Papeete. The Sandringham then found a new role, providing TAI passengers landing at Papeete aboard the airline's DC-8 jets with onward flights to Huahine, Tikihau, Raiatea, and Rangiroa in the Society Islands. A stopover of almost four hours was made at the atoll of Rangiroa. Passengers were taken ashore to the tiny village of Tiputa, where lunch was served at the Club Mediterranea and swimming facilities were available. After its passenger-carrying duties came to an end the Sandringham remained with TAI on standby for emergency rescue flights, finally making its last sortie, a search and rescue mission out of Tahiti, on 29 September 1970.

# 9

# SOUTH AMERICAN OPERATIONS

Jose Alberto Dodero was the owner of various shipping concerns in Argentina and neighbouring Paraguay prior to setting up his own airline, named Dodero, in 1945. After the war in Europe ended he paid a visit to Short Bros in Belfast, which led to the first airline order for their Short Sandringham flying boat. Four examples were purchased at a total cost of US$1,250,000 for use on proposed new routes across the River Plate. Two were to be completed as Sandringham 2s, with accommodation for twenty-eight passengers on the lower deck and a further seventeen on the upper deck, which also housed a cocktail bar. These machines were intended for use on the airline's shorter routes. The other two examples were to service longer routes, including those to Natal and Bathurst, and were to be Sandringham 3s, seating just twenty-one passengers on the lower deck, with a dining room and bar upstairs. All four aircraft were to be powered by Pratt & Whitney Twin wasp radial engines. At the time the order was placed Dodero had still to secure the necessary traffic rights, but construction proceeded anyway, and on 1 November 1945 the first example was named *Argentina* by Señora de Dodero and launched at Belfast. Temporarily registered as G-AGPZ for the ferry flight, the aircraft set off for South America on 19 November and arrived in Buenos Aires two days later after stops at Lisbon, Bathurst, Natal, and Rio de Janeiro. An order for a fifth aircraft was placed, but the delivery position was then sold on.

With all four Sandringhams safely moored in Buenos Aires, Señor Dodero was still battling to secure permission to operate his proposed routes. In a move to overcome this hurdle, in May 1946 he became one of the founders of a new airline called Aviacion del Litoral Fluvial Argentino (ALFA),

Short Sandringham G-AGPZ on a pre-delivery flight in 1945 before being ferried to the Argentinian airline Dodero to serve as LV-AAO. (via Raul)

and transferred ownership of the Sandringhams to this company. On 8 January 1947 ALFA was able to launch services, using the two Sandringham 2s on a routeing that followed the course of the Parana River northwards to Parana, Corrientes, Formosa and the Paraguayan capital Asuncion. Another route followed the Uruguay River to Concordia before continuing over land to Posadas. The Sandringhams also operated between Buenos Aires and Montevideo, and to Punta del Este in Uruguay in the summer months. Señor Dodero had hopes of obtaining traffic rights to Europe for ALFA, but these were awarded instead to the Argentine state-owned airline FAMA. He did gain some satisfaction when FAMA was obliged to charter ALFA Sandringhams to operate some of these services during the period June–September 1946, and in the course of one of these flights the ALFA Sandringham LV-AAR *Brazil* became the first Argentine-registered aircraft to cross the Atlantic on a commercial service, flying from Buenos Aires to Bicarosse in France via Rio de Janeiro, Natal and Bathurst on 4 July 1946. In November 1946 ALFA acquired another Sandringham 2, LV-ACT *Paraguay*,

Aerolineas Argentinas Short Sandringham LV-AAQ. (via Raul)

A taxiing shot of ALFA Short Sandringham LV-AAS. (via Raul)

but this addition to the fleet was balanced out by the loss of LV–AAP *Uruguay* in an accident on 29 July 1948. During that year ALFA placed an order for three civilianised Short Sunderland Vs, configured for fifty-one passengers, but before they could be delivered all of Argentina's privately owned airlines were nationalised in May 1949 and merged to become Aerolineas Argentinas, which was formally established on 7 December 1950.

On its formation Aerolineas Argentinas inherited a mixed fleet of landplanes plus the Sandringham flying boats. The state airline initially wanted

Aerolineas Argentinas Short Sandringham LV-AAO *Argentina*. (via Raul)

to withdraw these as quickly as practicable, but they were seen to perform
so well on the services across the River Plate that they were retained for this
purpose. On the route between Buenos Aires and Montevideo they operated
alongside the Sandringhams of the Uruguayan airline CAUSA, and the
shortage of suitable land airports in the region was to ensure their continued
use for some years to come. Three round trips each week linked Buenos Aires
to Concordia, and also to Posadas, the 500 miles to Posadas being covered
in a scheduled time of three hours twenty minutes. Seasonal flights were
operated to Punta del Este in Uruguay, and the aircraft also flew to Corriente,
and to Asuncion and Conception in Paraguay. When the Scandinavian airline
SAS terminated its flying boat operations in 1955 Aerolineas Argentinas
acquired that company's last example, a Sandringham 6 that, in 1946, had
been the last Short Sunderland to be civilianised for airline use. Throughout
its history Aerolineas Argentinas was to operate nine Sandringhams in total. In
January 1957 Sandringham schedules to Rosario were introduced, with three
round trips each week, but on the last day of that year one of the fleet was
lost in an accident. Shortly after departure from Buenos Aires LV-AAR *Brazil*
suffered an engine failure. Her crew elected to return to base but were then

Aerolineas Argentinas Short Sandringham LV-ACT *Paraguay*. (via Raul)

forced to attempt a landing in rough seas. The aircraft bounced on contact with the water and sank with the loss of nine lives. On 11 February 1959 another Sandringham was written off, this time without fatalities, when LV-AHG *Uruguay* sank whilst alighting at Montevideo.

By the end of the 1950s new land airports were being constructed, and new local service airlines had been formed to make use of them. In 1959 Aerolineas Argentinas announced its intention to retire its flying boats in April 1960. This provoked anxious responses from communities who feared they would be left without air links, and so initially the airline only withdrew the Sandringhams from the trunk route between Buenos Aires and Montevideo. On 1 May 1962 Aerolineas Argentinas finally ceased all flying boat operations. The five surviving Sandringhams were placed into storage at Puerto Nueve, Buenos Aires, until a new concern called Cooperativa Argentina de Aeronavegantes took them over, along with their associated repair shops and three launches, in 1963. The aim was to revive flying boat services in Argentina, and some flights were operated from December 1963, but the venture was not a success, and financial problems led to the cessation of all flying by mid 1964. During 1966 work was carried out on Sandringham LV-AAO to prepare it for operation as a freighter, but this did not happen. The Sandringhams gradually rotted at Puerto Nueve until they were broken up in 1967.

On the other side of the River Plate the Uruguayan airline Compania Aeronautica Uruguaya SA (CAUSA) had been set up in 1936 to provide air links between Montevideo and Buenos Aires. In the years immediately after the Second World War Junkers Ju 52/3m floatplanes were operated, but then the airline was offered two new Short Sandringhams by the British government. The first one, CX-AFA, entered service on 16 April 1946. The two original aircraft were later joined by another example purchased from the Argentine airline ALFA, and the trio settled into a routine of services between Montevideo and Buenos Aires twice each weekday, one flight each weekday between Colonia and Buenos Aires, and summer-only flights to Punta de Este. During its operational life the CAUSA fleet was to suffer its fair share of accidents and wear and tear, and in 1951 two surplus BOAC Sandringhams were acquired and placed into service as fifty-two-seaters. When Aerolineas Argentinas ended its flying boat services in 1962 it ceased to be viable for CAUSA to continue to maintain the marine aircraft bases in Montevideo and Buenos Aires purely for its own flights. The airline had already introduced Curtiss C-46 landplanes between these points, and on 30 April 1962 CX-ANI operated the last scheduled commercial flying boat service across the River Plate. CAUSA had been operating marine aircraft between Montevideo and Buenos Aires since 1938. The Sandringhams languished in the harbour at Montevideo until they were eventually broken up. The flying boat terminal building there survived for some time afterwards, being utilised as the harbour office.

# 10

# NORWEGIAN COASTAL SERVICES

Before the major Scandinavian airlines were amalgamated to form the Scandinavian Airlines System (SAS) in 1951, the national airline of Norway was Det Norske Luftfartselskap (DNL). The scarcity of suitable land airports along Norway's long coastline meant that flying boats would be needed in the short term to restore commercial services to the far north of the country in the aftermath of the Second World War. DNL accordingly placed an order for three Short Sandringham 6 aircraft to enter service from 1947. These were allocated the registrations and names LN-IAU *Bomse Brakar*, LN-IAV *Kritbjorn*, and LN-IAW *Bukken Bruse*. They were powered by Pratt & Whitney Twin Wasp piston engines and configured to carry thirty-seven passengers on two decks, with a galley on the lower deck. A crew of seven was carried on each aircraft, and to assist with navigation amongst the cliffs and mountains along the route the aircraft retained the ASV.6c radar of the Sunderland Vs, from which they had been converted. When services commenced in 1947 the aircraft had to be moored to buoys and the passengers and cargo transferred to them by small boats, but later on piers were constructed to simplify the procedure. Before each take-off or landing a watchboat would carry out a sweep of the area, looking for floating debris. The schedules were normally carried out by two of the Sandringhams, operating in opposite directions, with the third aircraft held in reserve. The northbound service departed from Sola, Stavanger, at 0600hrs and arrived at Bergen one hour later. On the next leg the flying boat threaded its way through the mountains on the two-hour journey to the seaplane base just outside Oslo's Fornebu Airport. After a crew change here the aircraft was airborne again an hour later, flying over land to Trondheim and onwards to

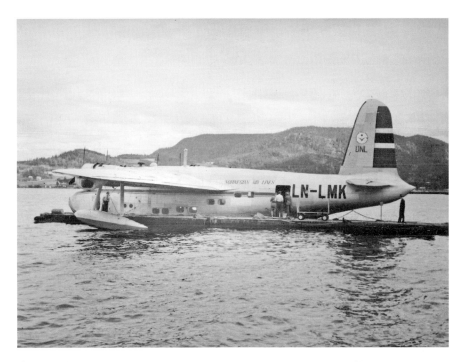

Short Sandringham LN-LMK of the Norwegian airline DNL. (Anthony Leyfeldt)

Brønnøysund, Sandnessjøen, Bodø, and Harstad, before alighting at Tromsø in the Arctic Circle at 1750hrs. From here, connections to Kirkenes were available, using Ju 52/3m floatplanes. On the following day the Sandringham retraced its journey southbound, setting off at 0700hrs and eventually arriving back at Sola at 1845hrs. During the winter months the danger of sea ice, coupled with several weeks of almost continual darkness, rendered the operation of the flights too hazardous and so the service only ran between late March and early October each year.

After the first season the stops at Brønnøysund and Sandnessjøen were eliminated, but despite its limitations the coastal service quickly became very popular, with the services usually fully booked. In addition to passengers the Sandringhams could also accommodate up to 2 tons of mail or freight. Cargo loads on the southbound schedule frequently included live polar bears, caught in the Arctic regions and bound for zoos in Europe. The flying boats built up a reputation for reliability, despite being unsuited to operations along Norway's more or less unsheltered coastline, but all three of the original aircraft were to be lost in accidents. One of these involved LN-IAW, on which the philosopher and author Bertram Russell was one of the surviving passengers. Two more Sandringhams, LN-MAI and LN-LMK, were acquired as replacements in April 1948 and June 1949. In addition to the scheduled services the aircraft were also used for popular 'midnight sun' excursion flights. By the time DNL was absorbed into SAS in 1951 land airports had been constructed along the coastal route, and flying boat operations soon ceased.

# 11

# PRESERVED FLYING BOATS

## Short Sandringham. Construction number SH974

This aircraft was originally delivered to the RAF in 1944 as a Short
Sunderland III with the serial number ML814. It was later modified to
Sunderland V standard and used by 330 Squadron on airline-type scheduled
services out of Sola in Norway to Oslo, Bergen, Trondheim and Tromsø
during the summer of 1945, pending the re-establishment of civil airline
services. After conversion to a Short Sandringham it served in Australia with
Ansett Flying Boat Services as VH-BRF *Islander* until that the Ansett flying
boats were withdrawn in 1974. The two Sandringhams operated by Ansett
were then bought by veteran US aviator Charles Blair for his new US Virgin
Islands-based airline, Antilles Air Boats. On 25 September 1974 *Islander*
departed Sydney on its delivery flight across the Pacific, the US mainland,
and the Caribbean to its new home at St Croix. Here it was registered
in the USA as N158J and given the new name *Excalibur VIII*. However,
from that point Antilles Air Boats ran foul of the US licensing authorities.
Because the aircraft's conversion to a Sandringham had not been carried
out by the manufacturer it was regarded as a non-standard modification,
and the authorities refused to allow it to be operated in US territory. The
flying boat was ferried to a disused US Navy base at Isla Grande in Puerto
Rico, where she lay neglected in a hangar until 1978. In September of that
year wealthy English businessman and flying boat enthusiast Edward Hulton
heard about the aircraft and contacted Antilles Air Boats with a view to
purchasing it, only to be told that Charles Blair had died that very day in

Sandringham F-OBIP. Musée de l'Air et de l'Espace store, Dugny, Paris, in 2002. This aircraft is under long-term rebuild and can only be viewed at the annual museum store and workshops open day. (Paul Middleton)

a flying accident. Shortly after that, Antilles Air Boats went out of business. The flying boat deteriorated, and the local authorities threatened to sell it as scrap to pay overdue base charges. However, a casino chain then acquired Charles Blair's business interests, and entrusted Ron Gillies, the former chief pilot of Antilles Air Boats, with the task of trying to find buyers for *Excalibur VIII* and the company's other Sandringham. In the meantime, Edward Hulton had let matters lie for a while, but in May 1979 he travelled out to the Caribbean and purchased *Excalibur VIII* from the casino chain. He set up an American company as the registered owner of the aircraft, which by then was in a sorry state, and arranged for a Miami-based aviation organisation to restore it to airworthy condition.

After more than a year's work the Sandringham was relaunched, and successful taxiing trials took place, but the US authorities were still adamant that they would not allow it to fly, apart from a one-off ferry flight to a foreign territory. For the next four months *Excalibur VIII* was moored in various non-US harbours while its new owners tried to find an airworthiness authority willing to permit it to fly in their country, and at the same time

Solent ZK-AMO. Museum of
Transport and Technology,
Auckland, New Zealand, 1995.
(Paul Middleton)

tried to recruit a suitably qualified crew for it. Eventually they decided that its best prospects lay in the UK or another European country, and Captain Bryan Monkton (formerly the founder of Trans-Oceanic Airways) was hired to undertake the transatlantic ferry flight.

As part of the preparations long-range fuel tanks were installed, and on 27 March 1981 the flying boat departed St Croix on the six-and-a-half-hour first leg to Bermuda. During that flight certain problems came to light that delayed the onward journey for many weeks, and it was not until 16 May that the aircraft was able to continue. The northerly routeing across the Atlantic via Gander, Newfoundland was selected, and on the morning of 18 May the Sandringham alighted safely on Lough Derg on the River Shannon in Ireland. On 21 May it flew onwards to the former RAF flying boat base at Calshot in southern England, also the base at that time of N158C, the other Sandringham formerly operated by Antilles Air Boats, and for the first time in almost thirty years two four-engined flying boats could be seen together at this historic location. This was to last for only a few days, however, as N158J soon departed for a new base at Marignane, near Marseilles in France. This location had been chosen as it still retained flying boat facilities, being used by locally based Canadair 'water bombers' for fighting forest fires, as well as being conveniently close to Edward Hulton's home in Monte Carlo. Once the Sandringham's support equipment had arrived the aircraft was brought ashore and spent more than a year in Aerospatiale's large hangar at Marignane undergoing corrosion treatment and repainting, which included the application of her former name *Islander*.

While this work was being carried out the decision was taken to take the aircraft to England and obtain a UK Certificate of Airworthiness. To this end, ownership of the Sandringham was transferred to a UK company called Sunderland Ltd. The UK registration G-BJHS was allocated to the aircraft, which was henceforth officially described as a converted Sunderland as the Sandringham conversion carried out in Australia had been non-standard. Arrangements for the flying boat to spend some time moored on the River Thames in the heart of London were negotiated, and *Islander*'s former pilot Ron Gillies was brought over to command the aircraft on her flight to London. *Islander* departed Marseilles on 6 August 1982, the first time she had flown in over a year. In advance of her arrival it had been announced that the aircraft would be open for the public to inspect internally as well as externally to raise money for charities, but little thought had been given as to how the public would be transported from the riverbank to her mooring point. Eventually, a small boat was made available for this duty, but many people had to be disappointed, due to the great demand.

A search was carried out to find a suitable location where the aircraft could be brought ashore and maintained during the winter, and this resulted in the flying boat being flown to Calshot and brought up the slipway there. The UK Civil Aviation Authority had indicated that there should be no problem over the issuance of a Private Category Certificate of Airworthiness, permitting the carriage of non-fare-paying passengers, appearances at airshows, and the use of the aircraft for advertising and corporate hospitality purposes, once certain specified modifications had been carried out. Work was still under way on these in October 1984 when the local authority covering the Calshot area announced that the site was to be redeveloped and the flying boat would have to be moved. Luckily, an alternative base became available at Chatham in Kent. Part of the former naval dockyard had been earmarked for a maritime museum, and covered accommodation could be used there for the time being. The requirement for a locally based commander for the Sunderland led to Edward Hulton establishing contact with former British Airways and BOAC pilot Ken Emmett, who had flown RAF Catalina flying boats during the Second World War, and BOAC Solents and Sandringhams post-war, and was probably the only pilot in the UK still licensed to fly civilian flying boats. His agreement to captain the Sunderland was the beginning of a ten year association with the machine.

After several test flights G-BJHS, now renamed *Sir Arthur Fouge* after the designer of the Sunderland, departed Calshot at 1115hrs on 20 November 1984 for her new base at Chatham. Work on the modifications recommenced, but was dogged by technical problems and bad luck. On two successive test flights during 1985 and 1986 the aircraft suffered engine failures. In October 1987 she was wheeled outside for engine runs, only to be caught in a violent storm. Hurricane-strength gusts blew her onto one wingtip, causing severe damage. By mid 1989 the Sunderland was airworthy and ready to fly once more.

Talks had been taking place with the fledgling Irish airline Ryanair over joint operation of the flying boat, which was intended to become the centrepiece of a new flying boat museum at Foynes in Ireland while still remaining in airworthy condition for promotional appearances. Ryanair was anxious to get the Sunderland over to Ireland in time to feature at the opening of the museum, and sent engineers and materials across to England to speed up the work. Ryanair titles and logos were applied to the fuselage, and yet another new name, *The Spirit of Foynes*, appeared on the nose. The Sunderland was launched and made a test flight on 6 July 1989, but further engine problems delayed the issue of its Certificate of Airworthiness and meant that it did not arrive in Ireland in time for the opening of the museum. The aircraft was initially based on Lough Derg in Ireland, but it had only been there for a week or so when its crew took a telephone call from England advising them that 'Sunderland Ltd and Ryanair have been unable to reach agreement … return at once to Calshot'. The Sunderland was flown back the next day and brought ashore at Calshot, where, fortunately, the redevelopment plans had fallen through. The Ryanair markings were removed, and the name *Islander* once more applied to the nose. For the remainder of that summer the flying boat was kept busy on promotional work, participating in the West Malling Air Display on 28 August and overflying the start of the Whitbread Round the World Yacht Race on 2 September. In October 1989, thanks to the generous assistance of Westland Aerospace, the historic machine was taken from the water to spend the winter ashore at the former Saunders-Roe facilities at Calshot.

In December 1989 Edward Hulton put the Sunderland up for auction at Christies, but failed to find a buyer. It was maintained in airworthy condition, and flew again at Coningsby on 16 June 1990 and on demonstration to potential buyers in September 1991. Another attempt at a sale by auction conducted by Sotheby's failed to reach the reserve price of £300,000, and the aircraft slowly deteriorated at Calshot until the end of 1992, when US aircraft collector Kermit Weeks purchased it for US$500,000. He had plans to put it on display at his Fantasy of Flight museum at Polk City in Florida, and specified that he was to be part of the crew on its ferry flight to the USA. To prepare him for this he received training on the type from Ken Emmett, and in July 1993 test flights resulted in the awarding of a new UK Certificate of Airworthiness to the aircraft. On 20 July 1993 the Sunderland departed Southampton Water on its way to the USA, with Ken Emmett as pilot-in-charge and Kermit Weeks as co-pilot. The flying boat routed via Ireland, Iceland and Canada to Oshkosh, Wisconsin, where it took part in that airfield's famous fly-in. It was to remain at Oshkosh for a year or so while a seaplane ramp was constructed and other preparations made at the museum, eventually arriving there in August 1994. On 4 July 1996 the aircraft played its part in the build-up to the Summer Olympic Games in Atlanta, transporting the Olympic torch between Sarasota and Miami. In mid July 2017 the Sunderland was still in store at the museum but was not on public display.

Sandringham VH-BRC 'Beachcomber'. Solent Sky, Southampton, 1998. (Paul Middleton)

Although none of the four-engined Sikorsky S-42s survive, several examples of its smaller twin-engined sibling the S-43 'Baby Clipper' are preserved in the USA. NC16934, seen in 2012, has been restored in false US Marine Corps markings as a JRS-1 at the Pima Air and Space Museum, Tucson, USA. (Paul Middleton)

# Short Sandringham 4. Construction number SH55C

After operating the final flying boat service of Ansett Flying boat Services, its Sandringham VH-BRC was sold to Antilles Air Boats in the US Virgin Islands on 10 September 1974. After a repaint, during which it acquired the temporary US registration N158C and the name *Southern Cross*, it departed Rose Bay, Sydney, on 28 November that year for its long ferry flight to St Croix via Pago Pago, Honolulu, San Francisco, Fort Worth and Boston, arriving at its new home on 9 December. Here it was re-registered as

VP-LVE and used on occasional flights in the area until on 6 July 1976 it set off across the Atlantic, bound for Ireland and a stay on Lough Derg, where the actress Maureen O'Hara, wife of the Antilles Air Boats owner Charles Blair, had a summer residence at nearby Bantry Bay. On 19 August 1976 the Sandringham paid a visit to Belfast and four days later it landed at Poole in Dorset. The harbour authorities there refused permission for it to operate pleasure flights from there as intended, and so it was moved to Studland Bay, Dorset, where it carried out nine passenger flights before setting off back to St Croix on 28 August.

In September 1977 the flying boat was back at Lough Derg, from where it operated charter flights under charter to the Irish airline Aer Arann. It then crossed the Irish Sea to the former flying boat base at Calshot. Here its operator again encountered difficulties. The use of Southampton Water for pleasure flights was denied, and so these were carried out from the mouth of the River Beaulieu, seventeen such flights being operated before the aircraft once more returned home to St Croix.

In September 1978 Charles Blair was killed in a flying accident, and shortly afterwards Antilles Air Boats went out of business. *Southern Cross* was put into storage at Grande, Puerto Rico, where its condition slowly deteriorated. Eventually, its sale to the Science Museum in England was provisionally agreed and it was restored to airworthy condition for its delivery flight under the temporary registration N158C once again. On 9 October 1980 the Sandringham departed Puerto Rico and after stops at St Croix, Boston, Port Washington (New York), Oyster Bay, Sydney (Nova Scotia), and Gander it landed at Killaloe in Ireland. Here it spent three months awaiting approval to enter the UK, finally arriving at Calshot on 2 February 1981. After two months riding at anchor there it was brought ashore in April so that restoration work could commence. However, after protracted negotiations a new temporary base at RNAS Lee-on-Solent was agreed upon, and in July 1981 the flying boat was relaunched onto the water and taxied on two engines for the 5-mile journey there. It was then towed up the slipway and put into storage again for eighteen months.

In 1982 the purchase of the Sandringham was finally formally completed, with the Science Museum contributing £40,000 and a further £45,000 coming from the National Heritage Memorial Trust. The original plan was for it to be stored at the Science Museum's reserve collection at Wroughton in Wiltshire until a permanent home could be adapted to house it and put it on display. This measure was not adopted, however. Both Rochester Council in Kent and Southampton City Council submitted plans for a permanent display site, and the Southampton proposal was chosen. The elderly flying boat's next move came about on 1 March 1983 when it was transported by the Army to Berth 28 at Southampton Old Docks on a self-propelled barge. Once at Southampton it was partially dismantled and stored in a secure compound while a new £403,000 museum, initially called the R.J. Mitchell Museum, was erected to house the Sandringham and other historic aircraft with a local connection. While this work was taking place the flying boat was repainted back into its Ansett Flying boat Services livery as VH-BRC *Beachcomber*. The new museum, now known as the Southampton Hall of Aviation, was completed during 1983 and the Sandringham was installed inside on 27–28 August. Once the other exhibits had joined it and the displays had been set up the facility opened its doors to the public on 26 May 1984 and was renamed the Solent Sky Museum in 2005. The Sandringham forms the centrepiece of the many historic exhibits and is open for inspection inside and out. In late 2017, after a £64,800 grant from the Heritage Lottery Fund for the purpose, work was in progress on the museum's recreation of the interior of an Empire flying boat. This was to include a flight-deck modelled on that of the museum's Short Sandringham.

## Short Solent 3. Construction number SH1295

After the failure of South Pacific Airlines to commence operations in 1958 the company's Short Solent N9964F was sold to the Hughes Tool Company, owned by the eccentric Howard Hughes. It was kept in storage under armed guard at San Francisco harbour from 1959 until 1967, when it was evicted and towed to Richmond, California, for further storage. After several changes of ownership it was saved from the scrap merchants in December 1976 by Rick and Randy Grant, who purchased it for US$50,000. A restoration group called the 'Friends of Halcyon' renamed it *Halcyon* and began preparing it for a proposed flight to Honolulu in 1978. The planned flight did not take place, and the Solent was later painted up to play the part of a Pan American Airways Boeing 314 Clipper flying boat in ground scenes for the movie *Indiana Jones and the Raiders of the Lost Ark*. After filming was completed it was repainted in the original RAF markings it wore when delivered to No. 201 Squadron as Short Seaford 1 NJ203 in 1946. In July 1989 the non-profit organisation Flying Boat Seaflite announced plans to restore the Solent to

The forward fuselage of former Reeve Aleutian Airways S-43 N15062 was last used as a (non-flying) boat but is now preserved by the Alaska Aviation Museum at Lake Hood, Anchorage, Alaska. It is pictured in 2008. (Paul Middleton)

flying condition and use it to operate passenger charter flights around the San Francisco Bay area, but nothing seems to have come of this. In 2017 the aircraft was on display at the Oakland Aviation Museum in California, and guided tours of its interior were available on specified dates.

## Short Solent 4. Construction number SH1559

On 15 September 1960 the Short Solent ZK-AMO *Aranui* operated the final revenue flying boat service of the New Zealand airline TEAL, on the Coral route from Papeete to Auckland via Aitutaki, Apia and Suva. As the last Solent 4 in existence it was earmarked for preservation and placed into open storage at Upper Waitemata Harbour in Auckland. Serious restoration work by the Museum of Transport and Technology (MOTAT) began in the early 1980s, by which time it had been badly vandalised over the years. In 2017 restoration work was continuing, and the Solent could be viewed at the MOTAT in Auckland.

## Short Sandringham 7. Construction number SH57C

On 29 September 1970 Short Sandringham 7 F-OBIP completed its last flight for RAI, a search and rescue mission out of Papeete. It then sat moored in a lagoon near to the new Papeete land airport until its sale by Civil Aviation Papeete in 1975 to Douglas Pearson Jnr, whose father had flown the aircraft during its RAI service. His intention was to return the Sandringham to the UK and put it on display at Rochester in Kent, but this project collapsed in November 1975. He then offered to donate the aircraft to the Queensland Air Museum in Australia, who sent a party out to Tahiti to inspect the flying boat and assess the cost and difficulty of transporting it to the museum. Mr Pearson then received a communication from Civil Aviation Papeete, advising him that the Sandringham in its present location was hampering plans to extend the airport, and unless it was moved by 1 March 1976 it would be broken up and the pieces would be dumped in the lagoon. The Queensland Air Museum had inspected the aircraft and had judged that it would be impractical for it to transport it to Australia, but Mr Pearson was able to arrange a 'stay of execution' to allow other preservation possibilities to be looked into. On 1 November 1977 he wrote to the Musée de l'Air et de l'Espace at Le Bourget, Paris informing them that: 'We wish to confirm that it is our desire to see the aeroplane preserved, notwithstanding its loss to Australia. We would rather see its preservation in Paris than its deterioration and eventual destruction in Papeete.' The museum agreed to take on the Sandringham, and in April 1979 it eventually arrived in Paris, having been transported there by the French armed services. It was restored and placed on external display at Le Bourget, but was severely damaged during a storm in February 1984. It was then moved into a hangar for repair and further restoration. In mid-2017 this process was still ongoing and the aircraft was not on public display.

## Vought-Sikorsky VS-44 NC41881

Vought-Sikorsky VS-44 NC41881 'Excambian' was one of three examples constructed for American Export Airlines and was delivered in May 1942. Until the end of 1944 the aircraft carried priority passengers and cargo under contract to the US Army and Navy. From January 1945 until late in that year it operated scheduled services for AOA. After a lengthy period flying with several airlines it was purchased in 1967 by Charles Blair of Antilles Air Boats for passenger services around the US Virgin Islands.

It was damaged beyond economical repair in 1969. In 1976 it was donated by Charles Blair's widow to the National Museum of Naval Aviation in Pensacola, Florida. In 1983 it was transferred to the New England Air Museum on permanent loan, and shipped by barge to their premises in Bridgport, Connecticut. After a lengthy restoration programme, it is now on display there.

## The Foynes Flying-Boat Museum

A drive of about forty-five minutes along the N69 road from Shannon in Ireland will bring you to the Foynes Flying-boat Museum and the nearest you can now get to stepping aboard a Pan American Boeing 314 Clipper flying boat of the 1930s and 1940s. The museum is housed in what was once the four-storey flying boat terminal building. Inside you will find a 1940s-style cinema showing historic flying boat footage, the restored original radio and weather forecasting room, and a diorama of the Foynes flying boat base in its heyday.

When they discovered that none of the Pan American Clippers that used the base had survived the museum staff looked into the practicality of constructing a full-size mock-up of one of the passenger compartments to give visitors some impression of what it must have been like to fly in one of these machines. From this beginning the idea grew into the construction of a full-scale replica of a Boeing 314 Clipper. The funding for this ambitious project was eventually secured, and the work was carried out off-site in around ten months. The replica was then transported in sections to Foynes at night and reassembled there. It is now 'moored' alongside the museum building, enabling visitors to step inside and inspect the fully furnished interior.

# Appendix 1

# FOYNES FLYING BOAT MOVEMENTS DURING SEPTEMBER 1943

An extract from the Foynes Harbour Register for the first three weeks of 1943, as reproduced in modified form below, recorded at least one flying boat movement each day, with many of the aircraft spending one (and sometimes two) nights at anchor there. The operation of the Poole–Foynes 'shuttle' can be seen, with, for instance, BOAC Sunderland G-AGHW arriving from Poole on 5 September with passengers for transfer to Pan American's Boeing 314 NC18611 bound for Botwood and then returning to Poole with inbound passengers off the Clipper.

| Arr. | Dept. | Registration | Type | Operator | From | To |
|------|-------|-------------|------|----------|------|-----|
| 1 | 1 | G-AGEV | Sunderland | BOAC | Lisbon | Poole |
| 1 | 1 | G-AGEW | Sunderland | BOAC | Lisbon | Poole |
| 1 | 2 | G-AGHV | Sunderland | BOAC | Poole | Lisbon |
| 3 | 5 | NC41881 | VS-44 | American Export | Botwood | Pt Lyautey |
| 4 | 5 | NC18611 | Boeing 314 | Pan American | Botwood | Botwood |
| 5 | 5 | G-AGHW | Sunderland | BOAC | Poole | Poole |
| 6 | 6 | G-AGCB | Boeing 314 | BOAC | Lisbon | Poole |
| 6 | 8 | G-AGCB | Boeing 314 | BOAC | Poole | Lisbon |
| 6 | 6 | NC18609 | Boeing 314 | Pan American | Botwood | Botwood |
| 6 | 8 | G-AFCI | Short S.26 | BOAC | Poole | Poole |
| 6 | 7 | G-AGEW | Sunderland | BOAC | Poole | Lisbon |
| 7 | 7 | G-AGEV | Sunderland | BOAC | Poole | Lisbon |
| 8 | 13 | G-AFCI | Short S.26 | BOAC | Poole | Poole |
| 8 | 8 | NC18611 | Boeing 314 | Pan American | Botwood | Botwood |
| 9 | 10 | NC41811 | VS-44 | American Export | Botwood | Pt Lyautey |

| 10 | 10 | G-AGCA | Boeing 314 | BOAC | Botwood | Poole |
|----|----|--------|-----------|------|---------|-------|
| 10 | 16 | G-AGHW | Sunderland | BOAC | Poole | Lisbon |
| 11 | 13 | G-AGCA | Boeing 314 | BOAC | Poole | Lisbon |
| 12 | 13 | NC41882 | VS-44 | American Export | Botwood | Pt Lyautey |
| 12 | 13 | G-AGHX | Sunderland | BOAC | Poole | Lisbon |
| 13 | 15 | G-AFCI | Short S.26 | BOAC | Poole | Poole |
| 14 | 14 | G-AGHV | Sunderland | BOAC | Lisbon | Poole |
| 14 | 14 | G-AGER | Sunderland | BOAC | Lisbon | Poole |
| 14 | 16 | G-AGHZ | Sunderland | BOAC | Poole | Lisbon |
| 15 | 15 | NC18612 | Boeing 314 | Pan American | Botwood | Botwood |
| 15 | 17 | NC41881 | VS-44 | American Export | Botwood | Pt Lyautey |
| 15 | 18 | G-AFCI | Short S.26 | BOAC | Poole | Poole |
| 16 | 16 | G-AGEW | Sunderland | BOAC | Lisbon | Poole |
| 17 | 17 | G-AGBZ | Boeing 314 | BOAC | Poole | Lisbon |
| 18 | 18 | NC18612 | Boeing 314 | Pan American | Botwood | Botwood |
| 18 | 20 | G-AFCI | Short S.26 | BOAC | Poole | Poole |
| 18 | 20 | G-AGIA | Sunderland | BOAC | Poole | Lisbon |
| 19 | 19 | NC41881 | VS-44 | American Export | Pt Lyautey | Botwood |
| 20 | 20 | NC18611 | Boeing 314 | Pan American | Botwood | Botwood |
| 20 | 22 | G-AFCI | Short S.26 | BOAC | Poole | Poole |
| 20 | 20 | G-AGHV | Sunderland | BOAC | Poole | Lisbon |

# Appendix 2

# FLEET LISTS OF MAJOR FLYING BOAT OPERATORS

Imperial Airways/BOAC (all surviving aircraft transferred from Imperial Airways to BOAC on 1 April 1940).

| Constructor's number | Registration | Name | Fate |
|---|---|---|---|
| Short S.26 Empire | | | |
| S.795 | G-ADHL | Canopus | Scrapped at Hythe Nov. 46 |
| S.804 | G-ADHM | Caledonia | Scrapped at Hythe Mar. 47 |
| S.811 | G-ADUT | Centaurus | Transferred to RAAF Sep. 39 |
| S.812 | G-ADUU | Cavalier | Sank in Atlantic Jan. 39 |
| S.813 | G-ADUV | Cambria | Scrapped at Hythe Jan. 46 |
| S.814 | G-ADUW | Castor | Scrapped at Hythe Feb. 47 |
| S.815 | G-ADUX | Cassiopeia | Sank Sabang Dec. 41 |
| S.816 | G-ADUY | Capella | Sank Batavia Mar. 39 |
| S.817 | G-ADUZ | Cygnus | Sank Brindisi Dec. 37 |
| S.818 | G-ADVA | Capricornus | Crashed Macon Mar. 37 |
| S.819 | G-ADVB | Corsair | Scrapped Hythe Jan. 47 |
| S.820 | G-ADVC | Courtier | Crashed Athens Oct. 37 |
| S.821 | G-ADVD | Challenger | Crashed Mozambique May 39 |
| S.822 | G-ADVE | Centurion | Crashed Calcutta Jun. 39 |
| S.838 | G-AETV | Corolianus | Transferred to Qantas Sep. 42 |
| S.839 | G-AETW | Calpurnia | Crashed Habbaniyah Nov. 38 |
| S.840 | G-AETX | Ceres | Damaged by fire Durban Dec. 42 |
| S.841 | G-AETY | Clio | Transferred to RAF Jul. 40 |
| S.842 | G-AETZ | Circe | Presumed shot down Java Feb. 42 |

| S.843 | G-AEUA | *Calypso* | Transferred to RAAF Sep. 39 |
|---|---|---|---|
| S.844 | G-AEUB | *Camilla* | Transferred to Qantas Jul. 42 |
| S.845 | G-AEUC | *Corinna* | Transferred to Qantas Sep. 39 |
| S.846 | G-AEUD | *Cordelia* | Transferred to RAF Jul. 40 |
| S.847 | G-AEUE | *Cameronian* | Scrapped Hythe Jan. 47 |
| S.848 | G-AEUF | *Corinthian* | Crashed Darwin Mar. 42 |
| S.850 | G-AEUH | *Corio* | Shot down, Koepang Jan. 42 |
| S.851 | G-AEUI | *Coorong* | Withdrawn Feb. 47 |
| S.876 | G-AFBJ | *Carpentaria* | Withdrawn Jan. 47 |
| S.878 | G-AFBL | *Cooee* | Withdrawn Nov. 46 |
| Short S.30 Empire | | | |
| S.879 | G-AFCT | *Champion* | Scrapped Hythe Apr. 47 |
| S.880 | G-AFCU | *Cabot* | Transferred to RAF Oct. 39 |
| S.881 | G-AFCV | *Caribou* | Transferred to RAF Oct. 39 |
| S.882 | G-AFCW | *Connemara* | Burnt out Hythe Jun. 39 |
| S.883 | G-AFCX | *Clyde* | Wrecked Lisbon Feb. 41 |
| S.1003 | G-AFKZ | *Cathay* | Scrapped Hythe Mar. 47 |
| Short S.33 Empire | | | |
| S.1025 | G-AFPZ | *Clifton* | Transferred to RAAF Mar. 42 |
| S.1026 | G-AFRA | *Cleopatra* | Scrapped Hythe Nov. 46 |
| Short S.26 G Class | | | |
| S.871 | G-AFCI | *Golden Hind* | Withdrawn Sep. 47 |
| S.872 | G-AFCJ | *Golden Fleece* | Transferred to RAF |
| S.873 | G-AFCK | *Golden Horn* | Crashed Lisbon Jan. 43 |
| BOAC | | | |
| Short S.25 Sunderland III Hythe Class | | | |
| | G-AGER | *Hadfield* | To Aquila Airways Aug. 48 |
| | G-AGES | | Written off Co. Kerry Jul. 43 |
| | G-AGET | | Written off Calcutta Feb. 46 |
| | G-AGEU | *Hampshire* | To Aquila Airways Jan. 49 |
| | G-AGEV | *Hailsham* | Written off Poole Mar. 46 |
| | G-AGEW | *Hanwell* | Written off Surabaya Sep. 48 |
| | G-AGHV | *Hamble* | Written off Mar. 46 |
| | G-AGHW | *Hamilton* | Written off Isle of Wight Nov. 47 |
| | G-AGHX | *Harlech* (later *Harlequin*) | Withdrawn May 48 |
| | G-AGHY | *Hastings* (later *Hawkesbury*) | To Aquila Airways Jan. 49 |

|  | G-AGIA | Haslemere | To Aquila Airways Jul.48 |
|---|---|---|---|
|  | G-AGIB |  | Written off 130 miles south of Tobruk Nov. 43 |
|  | G-AGJJ | Henley | To Aquila Airways Feb. 49 |
|  | G-AGJK | Howard | To Aquila Airways Mar. 49 |
|  | G-AGJL | Hobart | To Aquila Airways Mar. 49 |
|  | G-AGJM | Hythe | To Aquila Airways Feb. 49 |
|  | G-AGJN | Hudson | To Aquila Airways Feb. 49 |
|  | G-AGJO | Humber | Written off Hythe Feb. 49 |
|  | G-AGKV | Huntingdon | To Short Bros Dec. 48 |
|  | G-AGKW | Hereford (later Hotspur) | To Short Bros Dec. 48 |
|  | G-AGKX | Himalaya | Converted to Sandringham 1. To Aquila Airways May 49 |
|  | G-AGKY | Hungerford | To Aquila Airways Jan. 49 |
|  | G-AGKZ | Harwich | Withdrawn Jan. 49 |
|  | G-AGLA | Hunter | To Aquila Airways Jan. 49 |
| **Short S.25 Sunderland V** |  |  |  |
|  | G-AHEO | Halstead | To Aquila Airways Jul. 48 |
|  | G-AHER | Helmsdale | To Aquila Airways Oct. 49 |
|  | G-AHJR |  | Loaned to RAF Jun. 46–Apr. 48 |
| **Short S.25 Sandringham V Plymouth Class** |  |  |  |
| SH.31C | G-AHYY | Portsmouth | Withdrawn Jun. 49 |
| SH.34C | G-AHZA | Penzance | Withdrawn Aug. 49 |
| SH.36C | G-AHZE | Portsea | Withdrawn Sep. 49 |
| SH.37C | G-AHZG | Pevensey | Withdrawn Sep. 49 |
| SH.38C | G-AHZB | Portland | Crashed Bahrain Aug. 47 |
| SH.39C | G-AHZC | Pembroke | Withdrawn 1952 |
| SH.40C | G-AHZD | Portmarnock | Withdrawn Aug. 49 |
| SH.41C | G-AHZF | Poole | Withdrawn Aug. 49 |
| SH.56C | G-AJMZ | Perth | Withdrawn Aug. 49 |
| **Short S.25 Sandringham VII Bermuda Class** |  |  |  |
| SH.57C | G-AKCO | St George | Withdrawn Aug. 49 |
| SH.58C | G-AKCP | St David | Withdrawn Sep. 49 |
| SH.59C | G-AKCR | St Andrew | Withdrawn Sep. 49 |
| **Short S.45 Seaford 1** |  |  |  |
| S.1923 | G-AGWU |  | Loaned for evaluation Nov. 45–Feb. 46 |

| Short S.45 Solent 2 | | | |
|---|---|---|---|
| S.1300 | G-AHIL | *Salisbury* | Converted to Solent 3. Withdrawn Dec. 49 |
| S.1301 | G-AHIM | *Scarborough* | Withdrawn Dec. 49 |
| S.1302 | G-AHIN | *Southampton* | Converted to Solent 3. Withdrawn Nov. 50 |
| S.1303 | G-AHIO | *Somerset* | Converted to Solent 3. Withdrawn Nov. 50 |
| S.1304 | G-AHIR | *Sark* | Withdrawn Dec. 49 |
| S.1305 | G-AHIS | *Scapa* (later *City of York*) | Converted to Solent 3. Withdrawn Sep. 50 |
| S.1306 | G-AHIT | *Severn* | Withdrawn Nov. 49 |
| S.1307 | G-AHIU | *Solway* | Withdrawn Aug. 49 |
| S.1308 | G-AHIV | *Salcombe* | Withdrawn Sep. 50 |
| S.1309 | G-AHIW | *Stornoway* | Withdrawn Oct. 49 |
| S.1310 | G-AHIX | *Sussex* (later *City of Edinburgh*) | Converted to Solent 3. Crashed near Southampton Feb. 50 |
| S.1311 | G-AHIY | *Southsea* | Converted to Solent 3. Withdrawn Sep. 50 |
| Short S.45 Solent 3 | | | |
| S.1294 | G-AKNO | *City of London* | Sold in Australia Dec. 50 |
| S.1295 | G-AKNP | *City of Cardiff* | Sold in Australia Mar. 51 |
| S.1296 | G-AKNR | *City of Belfast* | Sold in New Zealand Jul. 51 |
| S.1297 | G-AKNS | *City of Liverpool* | Sold to RAF Nov. 50 |
| Boeing 314A | | | |
| 2081 | G-AGBZ | *Bristol* | Returned to USA |
| 2082 | G-AGCA | *Berwick* | Returned to USA |
| 2083 | G-AGCB | *Bangor* | Returned to USA |
| Pan American Airways | | | |
| Sikorsky S-42 | | | |
| 4200X | NC822M | *Brazilian Clipper* (later *Colombia Clipper*) | Scrapped Jul. 46 |
| 4201 | NC823M | *West Indies Clipper* (later *Pan American Clipper* and *Hong Kong Clipper*) | Sank Antilla, Cuba Aug. 44 |
| 4202 | NC824M | | Destroyed Port of Spain Dec. 35 |
| Sikorsky S-42A | | | |
| 4203 | NC15373 | *Jamaica Clipper* | Scrapped Jul. 46 |
| 4204 | NC15374 | *Antilles Clipper* | Scrapped Jul. 46 |

| 4205 | NC15375 | *Brazilian Clipper* | Scrapped Jul. 46 |
| 4206 | NC15376 | *Dominican Clipper* | Destroyed San Juan Mar. 41 |

| SIKORSKY S-42B | | | |
|---|---|---|---|
| 4207 | NC16734 | *Pan American Clipper II* (later *Samoan Clipper*) | Lost near Pago Pago Jan. 38 |
| 4208 | NC16735 | *Bermuda Clipper* (later *Alaska Clipper* and *Hong Kong Clipper III*) | Destroyed by bombing Jul. 41 |
| 4209 | NC16736 | *Pan American Clipper III* (later *Bermuda Clipper*) | Destroyed Manaus Jul. 43 |

| Martin M-130 | | | |
|---|---|---|---|
| 556 | NC14714 | *Hawaiian Clipper* (later *Hawaii Clipper*) | Lost east of Manila Jul. 38 |
| 557 | NC14715 | *Philippine Clipper* | Hit mountain 100 miles north of San Francisco Jan. 43 |
| 558 | NC14716 | *China Clipper* | Sank, Port of Spain Jan. 45 |

| Boeing 314 | | | |
|---|---|---|---|
| 1988 | NC18601 | *Honolulu Clipper* | Sank at sea by naval gunfire Nov. 45 |
| 1989 | NC18602 | *California Clipper* (later *Pacific Clipper*) | Purchased by US War Assets Dept Dec. 46 |
| 1990 | NC18603 | *Yankee Clipper* | Sank, Lisbon Feb. 43 |
| 1991 | NC18604 | *Atlantic Clipper* | Purchased by US War Assets Dept 46 |
| 1992 | NC18605 | *Dixie Clipper* | Purchased by US War Assets Dept 46 |
| 1993 | NC18606 | *American Clipper* | Purchased by US War Assets Dept 46 |

| Boeing 314A | | | |
|---|---|---|---|
| 2083 | NC18609 | *Pacific Clipper* | Purchased by US War Assets Dept 46 |
| 2085 | NC18611 | *Anzac Clipper* | Purchased by US War Assets Dept 46 |
| 2086 | NC18612 | *Capetown Clipper* | Purchased by US War Assets Dept 46 |

| Aquila Airways | | | |
|---|---|---|---|

| Short S.25 Sunderland III | | | |
|---|---|---|---|
| | G-AGER | *Hadfield* | Withdrawn Jul. 56 |
| | G-AGEU | *Hampshire* | Withdrawn Mar. 53 |
| | G-AGHZ | *Hawkesbury* | Withdrawn Jan. 49 |
| | G-AGIA | *Haslemere* | Withdrawn Feb. 51 |
| | G-AGJJ | *Henley* | Withdrawn Jan. 51 |
| | G-AGJK | *Howard* | Withdrawn Jan. 52 |
| | G-AGJL | *Hobart* | Withdrawn Jan. 52 |
| | G-AGJM | *Hythe* | Withdrawn Jan. 52 |
| | G-AGJN | *Hudson* | Written off, Funchal Jan. 53 |

| | G-AGKY | Hungerford | Withdrawn May 53 |
|---|---|---|---|
| | G-AGLA | Hunter | Withdrawn Aug. 49 |

**Short Sunderland V**

| | G-AHEO | Halstead | Withdrawn Nov. 49 |
|---|---|---|---|
| | G-AHER | Helmsdale | Withdrawn Jan. 52 |

**Short S.25 Sandringham**

| | G-AGKX | Himalaya | Withdrawn Mar. 53 |
|---|---|---|---|

**Short S.45 Solent 3**

| S.1302 | G-AHIN | Southampton | |
|---|---|---|---|
| S.1299 | G-AKNU | Sydney | Crashed IOW Nov. 57 |
| S.1293 | G-ANAJ | City of Funchal | Withdrawn Sep. 56 |

**Short S.45 Solent 4**

| SH.1558 | G-ANYI | Awatere | |
|---|---|---|---|
| SH.1556 | G-AOBL | Aotearoa II | |

**Qantas Empire Airways**

**Short S.23C Empire**

| S.489 | VH-ABC | Coogee | To RAAF Jun. 40 |
|---|---|---|---|
| S.850 | VH-ABD | Corio | Shot down Jan. 42 |
| S.851 | VH-ABE | Coorong | To BOAC Nov. 40 |
| S.876 | VH-ABA | Carpentaria | To BOAC Jun. 42 |
| S.877 | VH-ABB | Coolangatta | To RAAF Jun. 40 |
| S.878 | VH-ABF | Cooee | To BOAC Jun. 42 |
| S.838 | VH-ABG | Coriolanus | Withdrawn Dec. 47 |

**Short S.33 Empire**

| S.1025 | VH-ACD | Clifton | Crashed Rose Bay Jan. 44 |
|---|---|---|---|

**Short S.25 Sandringham IV**

| SH.30C | VH-EBW | | Damaged beyond repair Jun. 51 |
|---|---|---|---|
| SH.32C | VH-EBX | Pacific Chieftain | To Barrier Reef AW Dec. 54 |

**Short S.25 Sandringham V**

| SH.40C | VH-EBV | Pacific Warrior | Withdrawn Jun. 55 |
|---|---|---|---|
| SH.41C | VH-EBY | Pacific Voyager | Withdrawn Jul. 55 |
| SH.37C | VH-EBZ | Pacific Explorer | Withdrawn Jun. 55 |

**Tasman Empire Airways**

**Short S.30C Empire**

| S.886 | ZK-AMA | Aotearoa | Withdrawn Nov. 47 |
|---|---|---|---|
| S.885 | ZK-AMB | Australia | Crashed, Bathurst Sep. 42 |
| S.884 | ZK-AMC | Awarua | withdrawn 1947 |

| Short S.25 Sandringham IV | | | |
|---|---|---|---|
| SH.30C | ZK-AMB | *RMA Tasman* | To Qantas Apr. 50 |
| SH.32C | ZK-AMD | *RMA Australia* | To Qantas Apr. 50 |
| SH.33C | ZK-AME | *RMA New Zealand* | To Barrier Reef AW Apr. 50 |
| SH.55C | ZK-AMH | *RMA Auckland* | To Barrier Reef AW Apr. 50 |
| Short S.45 Solent 4 | | | |
| SH.1556 | ZK-AML | *Aotearoa II* | Withdrawn Jun. 54 |
| SH.1557 | ZK-AMM | *Ararangi* | Withdrawn May 54 |
| SH.1558 | ZK-AMN | *Awatere* | To Aquila AW 54 |
| SH.1559 | ZK-AMO | *Aranui* | Withdrawn. Donated to MOTAT |
| SH.1296 | ZK-AMQ | *Aparima* | |

# Sources of Reference

Many publications have been consulted for information and cross-checking purposes, including the following books:

Coster, G., *Corsairville* (London:Viking, 2000)

Davies, R.E.G., *Pan Am: An Airline and Its Aircraft* (Twickenham: Hamlyn, 1987)

Frater, A., *Beyond the Blue Horizon* (London:William Heinemann Ltd, 1986)

Hodgkinson,V., *Beachcomber: The Story of a Sandringham* (V. Hodgkinson, 1989)

Hull, N., *Flying Boats of the Solent* (Kettering: Silver Link, 2002)

Hull, N., *Aquila to Madeira* (Kettering: Silver Link, 2002)

Jackson, A.S., *Imperial Airways and the First British Airlines 1919–1940* (Lavenham: Terence Dalton Ltd, 1990)

Lowe, D., *The Flying Boat Era* (Auckland: The Lodestar Press, 1978)

Norris, Geoffrey 'The Short Empire Boats', Aircraft in Profile Number 84 (Surrey,:Profile Publications Ltd., 1966)

*Merchant Airmen* (HMSO, 1946)

Phipp, M., *Flying Boats of the Solent and Poole* (Stroud: Amberley Publishing, 2013)

Quinn, T., *Tales from the Golden Age of Air Travel* (London: Aurum Press, 2003)

Rance, A.B. (ed.), *Sea Planes and Flying Boats of the Solent* (Southampton: Southampton University Industrial Archeology Group, 1981)

Sedgley, P., *Wings over the Solent* (Southampton: Southampton Hall of Aviation, 1985)

Sims, P.E., *Adventurous Empires: The Story of the Short Empire Flying Boats* (Barnsley: Pen & Sword, 2013)

Smith, P., *The Last Flying Boat* (Southampton: Ensign Publications, 1993)

Trautman, J., *Pan American Clippers* (Boston: The Boston Mills Press, 2011)

SOURCES OF REFERENCE

## Articles

*Flight*
*Aircraft Illustrated*
*The Imperial Airways Gazette*
*Propliner*
*Air-Britain Digest*

## Websites

Poole Flying Boat Celebration, www.pooleflyingboats.com
The Pan Am Historical Foundation, www.panam.org
Solent Sky Museum, www.solentskymuseum.org
Queensland Air Museum, www.qam.com.au
Foynes Flying Boat and Maritime Museum, www.flyingboatmuseum.com
Wings over New Zealand Aviation Forum, www.rnzaf.proboards.com

You may also enjoy …

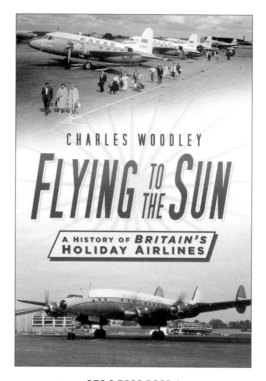

978 0 7509 5660 4

From humble beginnings flying holidaymakers to campsites in Corsica in war-surplus Dakota aircraft to today's flights across the globe in wide-bodied Airbuses, *Flying To The Sun* narrates the development of Britain's love-hate relationship with holiday charter airlines.

You may also enjoy …

978 0 7509 8583 3

Leading aviation writer Matt Falcus looks at the exciting airliners which can genuinely claim to have changed air travel, from the early mail planes and piston liners, through the emergence of the jet age to the sleek and ultra-modern airliners of today.

You may also enjoy …

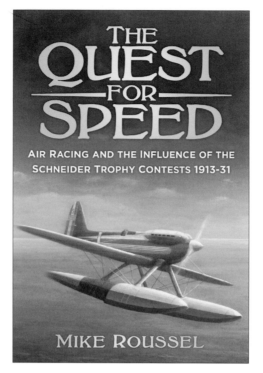

978 0 7509 6791 4

Most prestigious among air races was the Schneider Trophy, launched by French industrialist Jacques Schneider to promote the development of seaplanes. Eighty-five years since the British entry won the final trophy, this highly illustrated volume brings to life the 'quest for speed' once more.

The History Press

The destination for history
www.thehistorypress.co.uk